Character Education

Dealing with Frustration and Anger

Character Education

Character Education

Dealing with Frustration and Anger

TARA TOMCZYK KOELLHOFFER

CONSULTING EDITORS AND INTRODUCTION BY
Madonna M. Murphy, Ph.D
University of St. Francis
and **Sharon L. Banas**
former Values Education Coordinator,
Sweet Home Central School District, New York

CHELSEA HOUSE
PUBLISHERS
An imprint of Infobase Publishing

Character Education: Dealing with Frustration and Anger

Copyright © 2009 by Infobase Publishing

Chelsea House
An imprint of Infobase Publishing
132 West 31st Street
New York NY 10001

Library of Congress Cataloging-in-Publication Data
Koellhoffer, Tara Tomczyk.
  Dealing with frustration and anger / Tara Tomczyk Koellhoffer.
      p. cm. — (Character education)
  Includes bibliographical references and index.
  ISBN 978-1-60413-123-9 (hardcover)
  1. Anger—Juvenile literature. 2. Frustration—Juvenile literature.
I. Title.
  BF575.A5K65 2009
  152.4′7—dc22   2009001089

Chelsea House books are available at special discounts when purchased in bulk quantities for businesses, associations, institutions, or sales promotions. Please call our Special Sales Department in New York at (212) 967-8800 or (800) 322-8755.

You can find Chelsea House on the World Wide Web at http://www.chelseahouse.com

Text design by Annie O'Donnell
Cover design by Takeshi Takahashi

Printed in the United States

Bang EJB 10 9 8 7 6 5 4 3 2 1

This book is printed on acid-free paper.

All links and Web addresses were checked and verified to be correct at the time of publication. Because of the dynamic nature of the Web, some addresses and links may have changed since publication and may no longer be valid.

CONTENTS

INTRODUCTION

On February 14, 2008, as these books were being edited, a shooting occurred at Northern Illinois University (NIU) in DeKalb, Illinois. A former NIU graduate student, dressed in black and armed with a shotgun and two handguns, opened fire from the stage of a lecture hall. The shooter killed five students and injured 16 others before committing suicide. What could have led someone to do this? Could it have been prevented?

When the shooting started, student Dan Parmenter and his girlfriend, Lauren Debrauwere, who was sitting next to him, dropped to the floor between the rows of seats. Dan covered Lauren with his body, held her hand, and began praying. The shield of Dan's body saved Lauren's life, but Dan was fatally wounded. In that hall, on February 14, 2008—Valentine's Day—one person's deed was horrific and filled with hate; another's was heroic and loving.

The purpose of this series of books is to help prevent the occurrence of this kind of violence by offering readers the character education and social and emotional skills they need to control their emotions and make good moral choices. This series includes books on topics such as coping with bullying, conflicts, peer pressure, prejudice, anger and frustration, and numerous responsibilities, as well as learning how to handle teamwork and respect for others, be fair and honest, and be a good leader and decision-maker.

In his 1992 book, *Why Johnny Can't Tell Right from Wrong*,[1] William Kilpatrick coined the term "moral illiteracy" and dedicated a whole chapter to it. Today, as he points out, people often do not recognize when they are in a situation that calls for a moral choice, and they are not able to define what is right and what is wrong in that situation. The California-based Josephson Institute of Ethics agrees with these concerns. The institute states that we have a "character deficit" in our society today and points out that increasing numbers of young people across the United States—from well-to-do as well as disadvantaged backgrounds—demonstrate reckless disregard for fundamental standards of ethical conduct.

According to the 2006 *Josephson Institute Report Card on the Ethics of American Youth*, our children are at risk. This report sets forth the results of a biannual written survey completed in 2006 by more than 36,000 high school students across the country. The compilers of the report found that 82 percent of the students surveyed admitted that they had lied to a parent about something significant within the previous year. Sixty percent admitted to having cheated during a test at school, and 28 percent admitted to having stolen something from a store.[2] (Various books in this series will tell of other findings in this report.) Clearly, helping young people to develop character is a need of national importance.

The United States Congress agrees. In 1994, in the joint resolution that established National Character Counts Week, Congress declared that "the character of a nation is only as strong as the character of its individual citizens." The resolution also stated that "people do not automatically develop good character and, therefore, conscientious efforts must be made by youth-influencing institutions . . . to help young people develop the essential traits and characteristics that comprise good character."[3]

Many stories can be told of people who have defended our nation with character. One of the editors of this series knew one such young man named Jason Dunham. On April 24, 2004, Corporal Jason L. Dunham was serving with the United States Marines in Iraq. As Corporal Dunham's squad was conducting a reconnaissance mission, the men heard sounds of rocket-propelled grenades and small arms fire. Corporal

Dunham led a team of men toward that fire to assist their battalion commander's ambushed convoy. An insurgent leaped out at Corporal Dunham, and he saw the man release a grenade. Corporal Dunham alerted his team and immediately covered the grenade with his helmet and his body. He lost his own life, but he saved the lives of others on his team.

In January 2007, the Dunham family traveled to Washington, D.C., where President George W. Bush presented them with Corporal Dunham's posthumously awarded Congressional Medal of Honor. In the words of the Medal of Honor citation, "By his undaunted courage, intrepid fighting spirit, and unwavering devotion to duty, Corporal Dunham gallantly gave his life for his country."[4]

Thomas Lickona, the author of several books including *Educating for Character* and *Character Matters*, explains that the premise of character education is that there are objectively good human qualities—virtues—that are enduring moral truths. Courage, fortitude, integrity, caring, citizenship, and trustworthiness are just a few examples. These moral truths transcend religious, cultural, and social differences and help us to distinguish right from wrong. They are rooted in our human nature. They tell us how we should act with other human beings to promote human dignity and build a well-functioning and civil society—a society in which everyone lives by the golden rule.[5]

To develop his or her character, a person must understand core virtues, care about them, and act upon them. This series of books aims to help young readers *want* to become people of character. The books will help young people understand such core ethical values as fairness, honesty, responsibility, respect, tolerance of others, fortitude, self-discipline, teamwork, and leadership. By offering examples of people today and notable figures in history who live and have lived these virtues, these books will inspire young readers to develop these traits in themselves.

Finally, through these books, young readers will see that if they act on these moral truths, they will make good choices.

They will be able to deal with frustration and anger, manage conflict resolution, overcome prejudice, handle peer pressure, and deal with bullying. The result, one hopes, will be middle schools, high schools, and neighborhoods in which young people care about one another and work with their classmates and neighbors to develop team spirit.

Character development is a lifelong task but an exciting challenge. The need for it has been with us since the beginning of civilization. As the ancient Greek philosopher Aristotle explained in his *Nicomachean Ethics*:

> The virtues we get by first exercising them . . . so too we become just by doing just acts, temperate by doing temperate acts, brave by doing brave acts. . . . Hence also it is no easy task to be good . . . to do this to the right person, to the right extent, at the right time, with the right motive, and in the right way, that is not easy; wherefore goodness is both rare and laudable and noble. . . . It makes no small difference, then, whether we form habits of one kind or of another from our very youth; it makes a very great difference, or rather all the difference.[6]

This development of one's character is truly *The Ultimate Gift* that we hope to give to our young people. In the movie version of Jim Stovall's book of the same name, a privileged young man receives a most unexpected inheritance from his grandfather. Instead of the sizeable inheritance of cash that he expects, the young man receives 12 tasks—or "gifts"—designed to challenge him on a journey of self-discovery. The gifts confront him with character choices that force him to decide how one can be truly happy. Is it the possession of money that brings us happiness, or is it what we do with the money that we have? Every one of us has been given gifts. Will we keep our gifts to ourselves, or will we share them with others?

Being a "person of character" can have multiple meanings. Psychologist Steven Pinker asks an interesting question in a

January 13, 2008, *New York Times Magazine* article titled "The Moral Instinct": "Which of the following people would you say is the most admirable: Mother Teresa, Bill Gates or Norman Borlaug?" Pinker goes on to explain that although most people would say that, of course, Mother Teresa is the most admirable—a true person of character who ministered to the poor in Calcutta, was awarded the Noble Peace Prize, and was ranked in an American poll as the most admired person in the twentieth century—each of these three is a morally admirable person.

Pinker points out that Bill Gates made billions through his company Microsoft, but he also has decided to give away billions of dollars to help alleviate human misery in the United States and around the world. His charitable foundation is built on the principles that "All lives—no matter where they are being lived—have equal value" and "To whom much is given, much is expected."

Pinker notes that very few people have heard of Norman Borlaug, an agronomist who has spent his life developing high-yielding varieties of crops for third world countries. He is known as the "Father of the Green Revolution" because he used agricultural science to reduce world hunger and, by doing so, saved more than a billion lives. Borlaug is one of only five people in history to have won the Nobel Peace Prize, the Presidential Medal of Freedom, and the Congressional Gold Medal. He has devoted his long professional life and his scientific expertise to making the world a better place.

All of these people—although very different, from different places, and with different gifts—are people of character. They are, says Pinker, people with "a sixth sense, the moral sense." It is the sense of trying to do good in whatever situation one finds oneself.[7]

The authors and editors of the series *Character Education* hope that these books will help young readers discover their gifts and develop them, guided by a moral compass. "Do good and avoid evil." "Become all that you can be—a person of character." The books in this series teach these things and more. These books will correlate well with national social studies standards of learning. They will help teachers meet state standards for teaching social and emotional skills, as well as state guidelines for teaching ethics and character education.

Madonna M. Murphy, Ph.D.
Author of *Character Education in America's Blue Ribbon Schools* and professor of education, University of St. Francis, Joliet, Illinois

Sharon L. Banas, M.Ed.
Author of *Caring Messages for the School Year* and former values education coordinator and middle school social studies teacher, Sweet Home Central School District, Amherst and Tonawanda, New York

FOOTNOTES
1. William Kilpatrick. *Why Johnny Can't Tell Right from Wrong,* New York: Simon and Schuster, 1992.
2. Josephson Institute, 2006 *Josephson Institute Report Card on the Ethics of American Youth: Part One – Integrity.* Available online at: http://josephsoninstitute.org/pdf/ReportCard_press-release_2006-1013.pdf.
3. House Joint Resolution 366. May 11, 1994, 103rd Congress. 2d Session.
4. U.S. Army Center of Military History. *The Medal of Honor.* Available online at: www.history.army.mil/moh.html.
5. Thomas Lickona, *Educating for Character: Teaching Respect and Responsibility in the Schools.* New York: Bantam, 1991. Thomas Lickona, *Character Matters: How to Help Our Children Develop Good Judgment, Integrity, and Other Essential Virtues.* New York: Simon and Schuster Touchstone Books, 2004.
6. Richard McKeon, editor, "Nicomachean Ethics." *Basic Works of Aristotle,* Chicago: Random House, Clarendon Press, 1941.
7. Steven Pinker, "The Moral Instinct," *The New York Times*, January 13, 2008. Available online at www.newyorktimes.com.

WHAT ARE FRUSTRATION AND ANGER?

1

I was angry with my friend
I told my wrath, my wrath did end.
I was angry with my foe:
I told it not, my wrath did grow.

—*William Blake (1757–1827), poet*

Anger is an emotion that everyone experiences. It is a normal, even healthy, reaction to situations that one does not like. Anger itself isn't a bad thing. In fact, it can be a positive thing because it can give us the motivation needed to stand up and defend our values and beliefs. As psychologist Jan Luckingham Fable says, "Anger is meant to work for you, not against you. Anger is simply a signal that something is amiss." What *can* be a problem is the way a person deals with his or her anger.

Many things can make a person get angry. Experts refer to situations that provoke anger as "anger triggers." These can include the actions of other people or even yourself, as well as circumstances that make you uncomfortable or that you don't approve of. In general, a person's anger can be caused by anything that makes him or her feel threatened, whether that threat is a physical one or a threat to dignity, rights, or reputation.

HOW ANGER HAPPENS

As authors Glenn Schiraldi and Melissa Hallmark Kerr explain in *The Anger Management Sourcebook*, there are several things that happen when someone gets angry. First, he or she has thoughts that cause feelings of anger. For example, you might think that someone has treated you badly, or that you deserve something that you aren't receiving. Thoughts like that can begin the anger reaction, especially if a person thinks that whatever has happened to him or her was done deliberately or was unfair in some way.

Next, the body goes through some changes that let a person—and often other people, too—know that he or she is getting angry. The face may flush, the heart may begin to beat faster than usual, and the person may start to sweat.

Once the body gets involved in the anger response, the person begins to show certain behaviors. This might include raising one's voice, or even beginning to shout. Or a person might frown, pout, or clench his or her fists. At this point, anger can either become a useful tool, one that helps a person stand up for certain rights and get what is deserved; or it can be a problem, a dangerous reaction that can lead to fistfights, serious arguments, and even shattered relationships.

It is important to remember that anger is a secondary emotion. That means that a person *always* feels another emotion before he or she can feel anger. For instance, you might feel afraid, sad, or disappointed, or experience physical or mental pain. Anger is a reaction to that first feeling—a way to handle the emotions it brings.

EXPERIENCING ANGER VERSUS EXPRESSING ANGER

Everyone experiences anger at times; some people experience it more than others. It's unavoidable. There is a difference, however, between experiencing anger and expressing anger.

In the article "Anger Management FAQ: The Good, the Bad, the Ugly," Mayo Clinic social worker Robert T. Zackery explains that there are two basic ways to handle anger. One way is to express it. Expression can range from having a calm discussion with the person who is making you angry to exploding in an uncontrolled rage in which you risk harming someone or something, or even yourself.

The other way to deal with anger is to suppress it, or keep it inside. People who take this approach try to ignore or deny the fact that they are angry. They often think that showing others their feelings of anger or frustration will make them appear weak or out of control. Holding anger in can be dangerous to a person's health, causing high blood pressure, stress, headaches, and other problems. It can also be dangerous to relationships between people because someone who suppresses anger will eventually show anger in other ways. For example, people who try to keep their anger inside when they first feel it often hold grudges and therefore lash out at other people later. Many anger-suppressing people also engage in passive-aggressive behavior. This means they try to get back at other people in sneaky ways, such as purposely making someone late for an important appointment.

Most doctors and psychologists agree that the best way to deal with anger is to express it in a controlled manner that allows you to be assertive without hurting other people or yourself. As Robert Zackery emphasizes, the way a person deals with anger is a *learned* behavior. This means it is something you develop over time as you grow up and watch your family members, teachers, and peers handle their anger. As the psychologist Fable explains, "Knowing how to use anger to your advantage depends upon what you were taught within your family of origin." Because anger management is something a person learns, not something he or she is born with, it is possible to learn better ways to deal with frustration and anger.

THE THREE PARTS OF ANGER

Zackery, an expert in anger management, says there are three parts that make up the anger response. The first one is a psychological or emotional part. It is the emotion that someone experiences right before he or she gets angry. This is known as the primary emotion, and it might include sadness or fear. Anger, as explained earlier, is the secondary emotion.

The second part of anger is physiological. This refers to the way the body reacts to the feeling of anger. Among the most common physical responses are tightened muscles, a rise in blood pressure and heart rate, and the release of hormones, such as adrenaline.

The final part of anger is cognitive. This refers to the things a person thinks while angry. For example, some people may think that it's a normal part of life to feel angry. Others may think that it is essential to appear to be in control of their actions and emotions at all times; this can make them feel weak or guilty for being angry. The cognitive part of anger also includes the question of how a person thinks about anger over the long term, and whether someone holds grudges or is able to let go of the frustration and anger after experiencing it.

TYPES OF ANGER

Anger can take many different forms, depending on the trigger that causes it and the way the angry person responds. Psychologist W. Doyle Gentry, author of *Anger Management for Dummies,* surveyed a group of 284 people to ask them about their anger and the way they behave when they get angry or frustrated. From this data and his other research, he identified a number of anger "styles." These styles include episodic anger, chronic anger, and toxic anger.

According to Gentry, episodic anger is the kind of anger many people experience a few times every week when things just don't go their way. For example, you might feel angry if your sibling causes you to miss the school bus in the morning and you end up getting to class late and getting in trouble for it. Some 36 percent of the people Gentry surveyed said that they felt episodic anger. This type of anger lasts only a short while. It can spoil part of the day, or sometimes even the whole day, but it usually passes quickly—within a few hours or a day at most. The person doesn't continue to dwell on what happened long after the situation has passed.

In some people, however, episodic anger becomes more severe, Gentry writes. It turns into what he calls episodic rage. Those who have this kind of anger are the type of people Gentry calls "hotheads"—individuals who don't neces- sarily get angry often but whose anger is severe when it hap- pens. This type of anger can be dangerous to one's health.

Of the people in the survey, 11 percent said they expe- rienced chronic anger. Gentry describes chronic anger as a form in which the person gets angry several times every day, often as a result of the same triggers that occur over and over again. For example, people with chronic anger might get upset over a few different things each day: Perhaps they get angry in the morning when their sibling takes too long in the bathroom getting ready for school, and then they get angry again later in the afternoon while doing their homework because their computer's Internet connection is too slow. People who experience this kind of anger often think the way they feel is a normal response to frustrating situations and that they have their emotions under control. According to Gentry, however, getting angry every day is bad for the body.

Toxic anger, as described by Gentry, is any form of anger that is a risk to a person's health. Whether the anger surfaces as a short, intense bout of shouting, or is held in over a long period of time, it becomes toxic when it is dangerous to a person's body and/or relationships.

Therapist Kate Barcus Miller describes a few additional types of anger that are related to the person who feels the anger. One of her categories, described in her article "Anger Management: Anger Issues and Types of Anger," is sneaky anger. People who experience sneaky anger take care not to let other people see their anger. They feel that maintaining an image of control is very important. Because they hold their anger in and refuse to express it, they often have problems when their anger "leaks" out in other ways. For example, they may become forgetful or they may fail to do their chores or perform other responsibilities.

Miller also describes something she calls paranoid anger, which happens to people who have an unreasonable worry that they are being threatened by other people. They believe that others are "out to get them." They are always worried that other people are trying to take what is theirs, or trying to keep them from succeeding. Because of this, they might have a hard time recognizing other people's feelings, and they often think that the *other* people are the ones who are constantly angry. Their judgment is frequently confused, which can make it hard for them to get along with other people.

Another type of anger identified by Miller is shame-based anger. People who feel this emotion are extremely sensitive to criticism. They may need a lot of attention from other people in order to be happy. Deep down, they're always worried that they aren't good enough, and they rely on the way others treat them to let them know how they should feel about themselves. They often feel hurt and get angry when they feel like other people are ignoring them, even if, in reality, they aren't actually being ignored. This type of situation can make people lash out in anger, which can harm their relationships and make them feel even worse about themselves. This repeats a cycle of low self-esteem and angry feelings.

Psychologist Jan Luckingham Fable writes about another category of anger: historical anger. This form of anger is, simply put, the full effect of all the unexpressed anger that builds up over the course of a person's life. You add to your historical anger every time you suppress anger or frustration instead of expressing it in a constructive way. As Fable explains, "Historical anger fuels rage and, surprisingly, depression, too. It keeps you plugged into the past." When you live in the past, it is impossible to be present in the moment and enjoy whatever is going on around you right now. In order to lead a satisfying life, it is essential to find a way to let go of past anger and learn to enjoy the present. Fable writes, "Until an individual deals with historical anger, there is little chance that day to day situations involving anger will be handled with any degree of mastery. Annoyance, frustration, exasperation, feelings of being taken advantage of, or abused, or of being overprotected all stimulate the anger signal."

Finally, there is constructive anger, which writer David Foster describes in his article "10 Ways Angry People Change the World." According to Foster, anger can be used to give a person the energy and motivation to change the world in order to correct things that are unfair, unjust, or otherwise wrong. As Foster writes, "Things change. But whether they change for the better or not depends on what people do; not just any kind of people, but angry people." When a person gets angry, he or she feels a sense of being wronged and also a desire to right that wrong. If people are angry enough, they can focus all their anger on making other people aware of the situation they think should be changed. Often, showing others the situation can make them angry, too—angry enough to join the fight to change the world for the better.

ANGER THROUGHOUT HISTORY

The way society views anger has changed considerably over time. In particular, there have been many changes to the idea of how tightly people should control the expression of their anger. In their book *Anger: The Struggle for Emotional Control in America's History*, authors Carol Zisowitz Stearns and Peter N. Stearns examine the evolution of Americans' feelings about anger, from colonial times through the late twentieth century. They explain:

> Americans easily imagine themselves a rather angry people, heirs to a passionate past ranging from the righteous zeal of the Puritans who served a wrathful God, to Southern flashes of temper in defense of personal honor, through the quick-triggered Western frontiersmen with tempers to match. More recently, collective protest and widespread individual violence during the 1960s and 1970s reminded us that our history has been peppered with angry acts of force. . . .

Despite the fact that anger has played a large role in the history of the United States, the authors emphasize that Americans have been trying to find the best way to deal with their anger for centuries. During the colonial era, Americans were not nearly as concerned as people are today about whether expressing anger is a negative thing. In fact, as Stearns and Stearns write, "our founding fathers felt relatively free to storm and rage when the mood seized them and even took temper to be a sign of manliness." In contrast, "we have become embarrassed by such displays today."

This major change in the way anger is viewed and handled began during the middle of the eighteenth century. It happened in response to changes in the relationship between religion and government, the growth of democratic values, and the increase of literacy among the people. As Stearns and Stearns explain, literacy "produces a new sense of and desire for control, including a new interest in controlling anger. . . ." Also during this time, people began to view the family as being a safe haven from the problems and difficulties of the world, with its expanding economy and rapidly growing industry. Keeping anger out of family life became a major goal. Many people believed that keeping the family home an anger-free zone was necessary so

ANGER IN THE ANCIENT WORLD

Anger is an emotion that human beings have been struggling with for as long as they have been walking the earth. Throughout history, views of anger and how it should be handled have differed widely. In the ancient world, anger was a constant theme in both literature and philosophy.

In ancient Greece and Rome, poets, historians, and philosophers saw anger as something destructive, something that could easily bring about the downfall of civilization. In his epic poem *The Iliad*, ancient Greek poet Homer emphasized the power of anger from the poem's very first line. Throughout his work, Homer discusses the anger of both gods and men, and suggests that restraining one's anger is the best way to live in society. Hector, one of the characters in *The Iliad*, says, "I'll say that

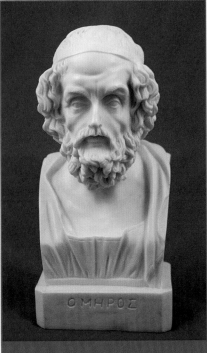

Greek poet Homer (shown in sculpture) knew how destructive anger could be and wrote of the importance of keeping anger at bay throughout his epic poem, *The Iliad*.

Agamemnon [another character in the poem] made me angry. However, what is done is better left alone, though we resent it still, and we must by force curb the dear passion [anger] in our breast."

Ancient Greek historians Thucydides and Herodotus said that anger hurts human relationships and prevents people from using reason.

(continues)

(continued)

Philosopher Aristotle considered anger a "sickness of the soul," writing that people "must show anger in the right way at the right time and at the right person." Roman philosopher Cicero echoed Aristotle's statement about expressing anger in a controlled and appropriate way. He said, "To govern one's mind and speech when angry is a mark of great ability."

that the family could continue to be a safe place where people could get away from the rest of the world. This changing view of the family and anger created new rules in society for how anger should be expressed—and even if it should be expressed at all.

Diaries written during the eighteenth century demonstrate that people were actively seeking to hold back their anger. The famous minister Jonathan Edwards wrote, "When I am most conscious of provocations of ill-nature and anger, then I will strive most to feel and act good-naturedly." As the eighteenth century gave way to the nineteenth century, many Americans came to believe that anger was an emotion that must always be struggled with and, if possible, controlled. This desire to keep one's anger in check has remained to the present day. Anger management training is available today in many workplaces, and the media often emphasize the potentially dangerous effects of anger on health.

THE BIOLOGY OF ANGER

Every time you get angry, you poison your own system.

—Alfred Montapert (1906–   ), writer

nger is an "emergency" emotion. It helps get a person ready to protect him or herself at times that might be dangerous. Anger evolved along with fear in animals, including humans, to make their chances of survival better when facing a threat. Anger is the body's way of letting the brain know that something is wrong. It tells a person that taking some action might be necessary in order to make things right.

THE FIGHT-OR-FLIGHT RESPONSE

Anger and fear are part of the so-called "fight-or-flight response." When someone faces a challenge of some kind—especially a physical challenge, such as being chased by a wild animal—that person's body prepares to either stand up to the threat and fight, or to run away from the danger. In threatening situations, anger gives a feeling of strength and power. That powerful feeling helps a person figure out whether to face the threat or flee from it.

Having anger as a protective emotion was very useful early in human history—a time when people were likely to face physical threats, such as life-threatening attacks from animals or other humans. According to Charles D. Spielberger, professor of psychology at the University of South Florida, "Fear and rage are common to animals, too, because it helps them to fight and survive." In the modern world, physical attacks and serious threats are rarer, but people still get angry. Unfortunately, many people tend to get angry about situations that aren't truly life threatening. As a result, the anger lasts longer than it should, and it can harm the body.

IS ANGER OUTDATED?

Anger developed in humans and other animals as a way to protect against attacks and other physical threats. In the developed world—such as the United States and Canada—few humans face these types of threats as often as people in ancient times did. Because of that, some scientists argue that anger is no longer useful. In today's society, instead of facing an attacking bear or mountain lion, most people deal with things that are merely annoying, such as traffic jams or stress at work or school. In other words, anger is designed to protect people from threats to their survival—not threats to pride or self-esteem. In a sense, civilization takes away anger's usefulness because there is really no way that anger can help when a boyfriend or girlfriend breaks up with you or when a classmate starts an argument. As Dr. Willard Gaylin writes in his book *The Rage Within: Anger in Modern Life*, anger "once may have served an adaptive purpose but now is only a potential source of trouble."

Because most people in the developed world hardly ever face real, life-threatening attacks, they often have trouble telling the difference between a real threat and a *perceived* threat—a threat that seems to be real but, in fact, is not. As a result, many people get themselves worked up into a state of anger to face threats that are nothing but figments of their imagination.

SHORT-TERM EFFECTS OF ANGER

When a person gets angry, the part of the brain that controls emotions releases neurotransmitters and hormones that are related to stress. The neurotransmitters and hormones enter the brain and the rest of the body and begin to do their work.

Adrenaline and cortisol are two of the hormones that are released. Adrenaline gives a person a burst of energy, which causes many changes to occur in the body. Someone who is angry breathes faster and may start to pant as his or her lungs work hard to take in more oxygen. Also, the body begins to sweat and the pupils of the eye dilate, or grow wide. The hormone cortisol affects the cardiovascular system, which makes a person's pulse rate and blood pressure level increase. The person may feel too hot or too cold, get goose bumps, and experience a tightening of the muscles. Also, when a person gets angry, his or her jaw tightens and his or her face turns red. Plus, the person may feel shaky or get a stomachache. Fat is released, bringing triglycerides—which provide the body with energy—into the blood. Blood flows to the parts of the body that need it most—those parts that will help the person stand up to the threat or run away from it. These include the arms and legs (which are responsible for fighting and running away) and the brain (which thinks faster so it can decide whether to fight or flee). Extra sugar, called glucose, is released into the blood to give the body energy. In a lot of ways, being angry is like being high on drugs. The angry person may have trouble thinking clearly and may lash out in violence.

Anger is supposed to be a short-term emotion, one that is meant to help a person deal with immediate threats that will be resolved quickly by either fighting or fleeing. After a person gets angry, however, the nervous system may remain excited for several hours or even a few days. Even as the body begins to come down from the angry state, there are more stress hormones in the blood than usual. This makes it more likely that the person will get angry again before he or she returns to a normal resting state.

LONG-TERM EFFECTS OF ANGER
Immune System Problems

Anger may cause the body to itch because a chemical called histamine may be released when a person gets angry. Histamines are produced when the body needs to deal with something that it is not used to. Among the most common things that make the body produce histamines are allergens—substances such as pollen or pet dander that cause an allergic reaction as the body tries to get rid of them. Histamines are produced when the body is trying to reject something that has gotten inside it.

When people get angry, they are basically "rejecting" something—whatever it is that is making them angry, whether it is a friend who has caused insult, or a sports coach who is being unfair to his or her players. As part of this "rejection," the body produces histamines. Over time, however, anger can cause the body to have trouble recognizing all of its tissues as part of the body, and the immune system may reject parts of the body itself. When this happens, the person may get sick easily because the immune system is not working at full strength. Anger that lasts a long time may also cause autoimmune disorders, such as lupus. These are sometimes fatal illnesses in which the immune system attacks the body's own tissues.

A study done over a period of 25 years at a Western Electric factory in Chicago compared angry people with people who didn't get angry very often. The study found that the angry, aggressive people did, in fact, have weaker immune systems than the less angry people. The angry people also had higher risks of dying from cancer and heart disease.

Heart Disease

Anger can have many serious, long-term, negative effects on a person's health. People who get angry often will constantly have their stress hormones at higher-than-normal levels. This can lead to a number of long-term health problems, especially heart disease.

According to Duke University psychiatry professor Dr. Redford Williams, "Getting angry is like taking a small dose of slow-acting poison." When someone gets angry, his or her brain causes large amounts of adrenaline and cortisol to be released. As was mentioned earlier, this causes the heart to beat faster and harder and raises the blood pressure. When blood pressure gets higher, a group of cells in one of the coronary arteries slowly weakens and breaks down because so much blood is swirling over it all the time. Adrenaline also makes the body release fat cells into the blood. These cells travel to the damaged artery to try to help fix it. If this continues to happen over a period of years, the fat cells may form a blockage that stops the flow of blood to the heart.

Studies have shown that anger causes other heart problems as well. In May 2000, researchers at Ohio State University discovered that angry people have higher levels of a chemical called homocysteine, which is linked to coronary heart disease. Homocysteine comes from animal protein and can damage the cells that line the walls of arteries. The study looked at 31 healthy men and 33 healthy women. These people filled out questionnaires about how angry they were and the ways in which they expressed their anger. They also gave blood samples, which the researchers used to measure their levels of homocysteine. The results showed that both men and women had higher levels of homocysteine in their blood when they suffered from chronic anger.

Although scientists do not yet know why anger increases homocysteine, they believe it is produced when the sympathetic nervous system is turned on. (The sympathetic nervous system is part of the automatic nervous system—the part that handles reactions we can't consciously control, such as the fight-or-flight response.) In angry people, the sympathetic nervous system is always in an "alert" state.

Anger is closely related to most forms of heart disease. Heart attacks are the number one cause of death in the United States, so chronic anger is a serious problem. When a person becomes angry, the heart rate can go up to 180 beats per minute or more. The average normal heart rate is around 80 beats per minute. Blood pressure shoots up to 220 over 130 or more, as opposed to the normal rate of about 120 over 80. When heart rate and blood pressure increase, the body thinks it's in danger of injury or death. To protect the person, the body releases chemicals that help make the blood clot, or stick together, to keep the person from bleeding to death if he or she does in fact get injured. This clotting reaction is dangerous when there is no injury because blood clots can form and travel to the body's organs, including the brain or heart, where they can cause instant death.

During an angry outburst, another type of heart problem can occur. As the person's body responds to the perceived threat, the arteries can squeeze themselves closed hard enough to cut off the supply of oxygen to the heart. This can result in chest pain, known as *angina pectoris*. In some cases, it can even lead to a heart attack, which may be fatal. A severe fit of anger can also cause blood vessels in the brain to burst, which could lead to a stroke.

Angry people may be at risk of other diseases for reasons that aren't directly the result of their anger. In general, people who have chronic anger also tend to have poor health habits. They may eat too much junk food, smoke, or drink alcohol excessively. These are all bad habits that people may engage in to try to relax and soothe their anger. All of these behaviors also increase the risk of heart disease, so they make angry people even more likely to suffer heart attacks and related health problems.

OTHER LONG-TERM EFFECTS

Researchers have found connections between chronic anger and strokes, digestive problems, and respiratory (breathing) disorders. There is even a link between chronic anger and diabetes since the body releases large amounts of sugar into the blood when a person gets angry. The body can also suffer severe fatigue from being on alert all the time.

In addition to all of these physical problems that anger can cause, it can also result in mental health problems. Anger and depression are closely related. Many health experts believe that anger can help cause depression, and vice versa. The emotional pain associated with depression can make a person feel angry. At the same time, being angry all the time can result in exhaustion and hopelessness, which are symptoms of depression. A depressed person tends to have a negative view of the world, along with sleep problems, low energy levels, and a lack of self-esteem, all of which make it easy to get frustrated and angry even in situations that would not normally cause anger. Many depressed people who have gotten treatment have noticed that they don't get angry as often as they did before they sought help for their depression.

Anger and depression both act on a certain neurotransmitter in the brain: serotonin. A great deal of research has shown that a lack of serotonin in the brain is a cause of depression. Scientists now believe that chronic anger, too, may be caused in part by lower-than-normal levels of serotonin.

SITUATIONS THAT CAUSE FRUSTRATION AND ANGER

How much more grievous are the consequences of anger than the causes of it.

—*Marcus Aurelius (A.D. 121–180), Roman emperor*

Even the most mild-mannered person gets angry once in a while, and there are countless situations that might cause anger. In *Anger: The Struggle for Emotional Control in America's History*, authors Carol and Peter Stearns explain that there is one basic emotion that lies at the heart of almost all anger: disappointment. "We become angry when we are disappointed and particularly when we view the disappointment as unjust or unexpected," they explain. "This is one reason, perhaps, that recent research has shown that we become angry most often at those to whom we feel emotionally close—in fact, at our loved ones." Anyone who has had a big blowout of an argument with a brother, sister, parent, or close friend knows very well that it can be easiest to get angry with the people who are closest to you.

So what are some of the situations that can lead to frustration and anger? It is nearly impossible to mention every possible anger-causing experience or circumstance, but some of the most common ones include:

* Stress at work or school
* Crowds
* Being irritated or annoyed
* Anxiety
* Mood disorders (including depression, bipolar disorder, and borderline personality disorder)
* Being treated unfairly
* Loud noises
* Unpleasant weather, such as extreme heat or cold
* Hunger
* Lack of sleep
* Pain
* Being harassed
* Being threatened physically or emotionally
* Being forced to wait (for example, waiting in lines or waiting for someone who is late)
* Loss of control over a situation
* Personality (people with "type A" personalities, who are overachievers or perfectionists and tend to be in a rush to get things done, are often angry more often than others)

INTERNAL AND EXTERNAL CAUSES OF ANGER

Great Britain's National Health Service (NHS) offers a program called "First Steps," which offers information about mental health and other medical issues to the public. According to the First Steps program of anger management, there are two basic categories of situations that can cause anger: internal and external.

External causes are those that people would most likely think of when thinking about getting angry: things that other people do, or random and unfortunate events such as accidents. There are both short-term and long-term

THE LONG, HOT SUMMER EFFECT

During the late 1960s, it became common for riots to break out in large cities during the hot summer months. A study in the *International Journal of Law and Psychiatry* in 1999 found that the riots that occurred in 1967 all happened when the temperature was above 80°F (27°C). The study looked at 17 cities that had riots that summer, and in 15 of them, the temperature was very high when the riots happened. Because almost all of these riots took place when the temperatures were abnormally high, many scientists began to wonder whether high heat (or extreme cold) could actually cause anger, which then led to rioting. Several studies were done to test what some observers called the "long, hot summer effect."

In 1972, researchers R.A. Baron and S.F. Lawton conducted an experiment to measure people's reactions to temperature. They put people alone in rooms and told them that they could use a special dial to shock "the experimenter" in another room. The "experimenter" spoke through an intercom and constantly insulted the people who were being studied to try to make them angry. Baron and Lawton discovered that those people who were in rooms where the temperature was very warm gave the experimenter more intense shocks compared with those given by the people in rooms that weren't so hot. The researchers also found that the people in very cold rooms also gave the experimenter severe shocks.

Studies like this confirmed the belief that anger is intensified by extremes in temperature. Still, scientists wondered why riots always seemed to take place during the warmest part of the summer, and never during the coldest days of winter. Scientists at the University of Michigan thought about this and came up with an answer that made situations that can provoke angry responses. Short-term causes of anger might include a rude salesperson in a shop, an unfair referee call in a game, or someone cutting in line at the movies. These situations are called "short term"

sense: During the winter, when it is very cold, people don't often go outside. Instead, they stay inside where heating systems keep them warm. During the summer, however, people are more likely to be outdoors—especially people who don't have air conditioning in their homes. For these people, getting out in the fresh air is the only way to find some relief from the heat. If some people get in an argument, it is very easy for fights to break out, which can turn into riots as the entire outdoor crowd gets involved.

Studies have found that high temperatures intensify people's anger. A violent race riot in July of 1967 in Detroit, Michigan, lasted five days and resulted in 43 deaths.

because the offensive act is over almost immediately after it happens—although the anger a person feels because of it might last considerably longer.

Long-term causes of anger include situations that continue over a period of time, whether it is just for a few days or for many years. These situations might include a too-heavy load of homework at school, an ongoing disagreement with a sibling or a friend, or stresses over money or things such as whether you'll be able to get into college. These types of worries or problems tend to last for some time, and they can keep you in an almost constant state of anger or frustration, which can be very dangerous to your health.

Conflict resolution expert Tristan Loo writes in a 2005 article called "What Causes Anger?" about several internal and external causes of anger. On the list of internal factors is emotional reasoning, or how a person looks at everything when he or she is feeling strong emotions. Highly emotional people often have trouble interpreting the reasons why things happen and the motives of other people. This can make it easy for them to become irritated and, ultimately, angry.

Another internal cause that Loo describes is a low tolerance for frustration. No one likes to be frustrated, but some people are able to figure out how to change things so that the frustration either ends or they are able to handle it. People who overreact to frustrating situations get angry easily, and so they tend to make even minor disappointments seem like larger-than-life problems.

Loo writes that there are four general external sources of anger. These include:

* Personal attacks
* Threats to one's ideas or opinions
* Threats to one's basic needs
* Frustrating events or people

THE FOUR PRIMARY CAUSES OF ANGER

In *The Anger Management Sourcebook*, authors Glenn Schiraldi and Melissa Hallmark Kerr break down the causes of anger into categories. Unlike Loo or Britain's First Steps program, however, Schiraldi and Kerr define the categories as primary and secondary. There are four main causes of anger within the primary category.

According to Schiraldi and Kerr, the first primary cause of anger is the simple fact that human beings care about things: their lives, their loved ones, and the world around them. People always want to protect what is theirs and they want to be able to live and grow in the ways they choose. When someone or some situation threatens your well-being or the well-being of something or somebody you care about, you may become angry. As Schiraldi and Kerr put it, "If we did not care, we would cease to react."

The second primary cause of anger outlined by Schiraldi and Kerr is self-diminishment, which means a feeling of being a "nobody" or not being respected. Having a strong sense of self-worth and feeling that other people like and care about you is a big part of being happy. When someone rejects you or makes you feel small or weak, it is easy to get angry.

The third primary cause of anger is closely related to the second cause: People get angry because feelings of anger can help them feel less powerless, and can, at least for a while, overcome their feelings of self-diminishment. Anger is really just a form of energy, an emotion that gives people the power they need to fight for what they want or believe. Being angry can help a person feel higher self-esteem—but only for a short time. Eventually, you still need to address the person or situation that made you feel worthless to begin with.

Finally, according to Schiraldi and Kerr, the fourth primary cause of anger is unrealistic expectations. Although they may not realize it, many people expect quite a lot from the world and from others. Most people realize that nothing is ever perfect. Even so, they still expect public transportation to run on time, they expect everyone to do their share of the work when there is a group project, and they expect everything in life to go smoothly. Expecting all of this all of the time sets a person up for disappointment when things end up not going according to plan. As was discussed earlier, disappointment is perhaps the most common cause of anger.

SECONDARY CAUSES OF ANGER

Schiraldi and Kerr also point out several secondary causes of anger. These include the following:

- ❋ Hot buttons, which Schiraldi and Kerr define as "unhealed emotional wounds or unresolved pain from the past." Everyone has memories of times when they felt weak or not good enough. When something happens to stir up those memories, a person often feels the same disappointment all over again.
- ❋ Family/personal history, which means that you learn how to deal with anger from your family and the other people around you as you grow up. Whether you lash out in a violent rage or bottle up your anger inside of you depends a lot on the way your childhood role models behaved when they were angry.
- ❋ The thoughts people have about their anger, which can either ease their angry feelings or make the anger even worse. If someone sees the situations that make him or her angry as things that happen to all people, then the anger he or she feels will probably be short-lived and not very intense. If, on the other hand, a person tends to believe that the things that are causing his or her anger are being done on purpose, then that person's anger will probably be long-lasting and severe.

ANGER IN THE WORKPLACE

A nger has become much too common in many offices and other workplaces. Even in schools, it is not unusual to see tensions running high between students and teachers. Among the causes of anger in the workplace and in school are the following:

* Poor management/unclear instructions—in other words, not providing the employee or student with clear, detailed directions so he or she can complete the task well
* Unfair treatment by managers or teachers

(continues)

Teacher Samson Lyman talks to students outside Washington State's Moses Lake High School in March of 2007. Lyman (*left*) had been suspended from the school, in part for making derogatory remarks about a Mormon university. He was carried out of the school after bursting into the cafeteria and "initiating a riot," according to officials. Lyman later started protesting outside the school to continue his complaints of unfair treatment.

(continued)

* Lack of opportunities—in business, this means not enough chances to get promoted to a better job; in schools, this can mean a lack of extracurricular activities, or lessons that don't challenge the student enough
* Not being appreciated for a job well done
* Too much work or homework
* Dishonesty among coworkers or fellow students
* Incompetence—in other words, employees who aren't skilled enough to do their jobs correctly, or students who either can't or don't grasp the material being taught
* Rude treatment by coworkers or fellow students
* Power plays—in other words, managers or teachers who dominate workers or students under their supervision in unfair ways, as well as workers who consistently behave in ways managers consider unprofessional

* Too much focus on "the self," or being the type of person who expects things to go his or her way all the time. When a person thinks mainly—or only—of him or herself, it is easy for that person to get angry when other people don't do things the way he or she thinks they should be done.
* Social environment, which means the circumstances in which you live, including your family life and your work or school experiences. It also includes what you see in the media regarding violence, aggression, and anger. When the media make it look like going into a rage over imperfect situations is normal, it is easy for you to start believing your own angry behavior is normal.
* Lack of skills, meaning that some people have never learned the tools needed to thrive in society. These

tools include problem solving, how to face negative situations with humor and hope, and how to work well with other people.

❋ Biology, which refers to all the things that go on in the body that can affect how angry a person gets. For instance, having a healthy nervous system is essential when it comes to managing anger. If you're under too much stress or haven't been getting enough sleep, you might experience changes in the way your nervous system works. Certain changes can make it easier for you to get angry and keep feeling angry longer than you should.

❋ Not enough time to relax, which means lacking free time to rest, play, or engage in activities that improve both physical and emotional health.

❋ Mental illness, including schizophrenia, depression, and personality disorders, all of which can have anger as a symptom.

OTHER RISK FACTORS FOR ANGER

In *Anger Management for Dummies*, author W. Doyle Gentry lists a variety of situations and factors that can make anger more likely to happen. According to Gentry, taking drugs—either illegal drugs, prescription drugs, or even "mild" drugs such as caffeine—can change the chemistry of the brain and make it easier than usual to get angry. People who lack communication skills tend to get angry often, too, Gentry says, because they have a hard time letting people know what they want and expressing their disappointment when things don't go their way. Other risk factors for anger include being a judgmental person who always looks for the worst in other people and situations; being a "blamer," someone who thinks others are responsible for his or her problems; and not having enough supportive people around to help with problem solving or to give advice about dealing with disappointment and frustration.

4

DESTRUCTIVE USES OF ANGER IN HISTORY

You cannot shake hands with a clenched fist.
—*Golda Meir (1898–1978), former prime minister of Israel*

Like all emotions, anger is something that everyone feels at times. For some people, though, anger becomes more than a fleeting emotion that comes and goes. It turns into an obsession—something that takes over a person's life and becomes the reason behind their actions. When this happens, anger can lead people to commit violent and destructive acts that can change the world in terrible ways. In fact, destructive anger has been at the heart of many events that shaped history.

THE CRUSADES

The Crusades were a series of military campaigns that took place during the Middle Ages (around A.D. 400 to 1500). The Roman Catholic Church encouraged Christians to travel to the Holy Land and take control of the area away from the Muslims who lived there. Religious differences were at the core of the feud between Christians and Muslims, but anger also played a big role in launching the Crusades.

During the Middle Ages, devout Christians often took long and grueling trips, called pilgrimages, to the Holy Land. Christian pilgrims wanted to see for themselves the places where Jesus Christ had lived. After Islam spread through the Middle East in the seventh century, Muslims took control of key locations in the Holy Land and sometimes made it difficult for Christian pilgrims to visit sites that had religious significance in Christianity, such as the city of Jerusalem. Anger over Muslims' treatment of the Christian pilgrims—and, even more important, anger that Muslims were taking over lands that the Catholic Church believed should belong to Christians—led Pope Urban II to call for the start of the First Crusade in 1095.

Muslims responded to Christians' anger with anger of their own. The sites that Christians wanted to control were also important religious places for Muslims. The followers of Islam were determined not only to hold on to the Holy Land, but also to spread their faith to new places. What started as religious devotion on both sides—Christian and Muslim—quickly became a massive display of violence and anger that would last into the fifteenth century.

Although the Muslims ultimately succeeded in driving away the Christians, they developed a view of Christianity that continues to affect Muslim-Christian relations to this day. A key issue that drives the ongoing tensions in the Middle East—the creation of the state of Israel after the Holocaust, during which Nazi Germany persecuted and killed Jews—is often seen by Muslims as one more example of the Christians' attempt to take over the Holy Land (in the case of Israel, on behalf of the Jews). In his 2007 article, "Causes, History, and Violence of the Crusades," religious violence expert Austin Cline writes, "The Crusades exemplify the way in which religious devotion can become a violent act in a grand . . . drama of good vs. evil—an attitude which persists through today in the form of religious extremists and terrorists."

A violent scene from the Crusades is depicted here in *The Capture of Constantinople in 1204* by artist Jacopo Robusti. Anger between Christians and Muslims was a key cause of the Crusades.

MARTIN LUTHER: ANGER AND THE PROTESTANT REFORMATION

For centuries after the birth of Christianity, there was only one Christian church—the Roman Catholic Church—and all Christians were part of it. That changed in a dramatic way during the early sixteenth century, in large part because a man named Martin Luther got angry.

Born in 1483 in Germany, Martin Luther grew up and became a monk. Although he was a devout Christian, over time he began to notice some things he didn't like about the Catholic Church. What bothered him the most was the way some unethical clergymen, including a preacher named Johann Tetzel, were selling "indulgences." The Catholic Church defined an *indulgence* as pardon from punishment for a sin that has already been forgiven by God. Tetzel and other clergy, however, led the common people to believe they could buy actual forgiveness for their sins—not just pardon from punishment—by paying a sum of money.

Seeing the way these men of the church were abusing the trust of the people made Luther so angry that he decided to do something to try to fix the situation. In 1517, he wrote a long list—later called the Ninety-five Theses—that outlined his complaints about the Catholic Church. In addition to the selling of indulgences, Luther expressed his anger about the way the Pope—who was then very rich—took money from the poor to build new churches and cathedrals. Luther knew his anger was a powerful tool. He wrote, "I never work better than when I am inspired by anger; for when I am angry, I can write, pray, and preach well, for then my whole temperament is quickened, my understandings sharpened, and all mundane vexations and temptations depart."

Luther didn't intend to start a revolt against the Catholic Church. He only wanted to vent his anger and possibly get the church to make some changes for the better. Instead, Luther ended up winning the support of many people, from fellow monks to dukes and kings, who were also angry with the church for taking money and land from them as tax payments to the Catholic Church. Over time, their complaints—and Luther's—continued to grow, until they made a break with the Catholic Church and started a new

Martin Luther—depicted here as the focus of the painting *Burning the Papal Bull* by Carl Friedrich Lessing—was a major leader in the formation of Protestantism after he became frustrated with the corruption he saw within the Roman Catholic Church.

branch of Christianity called Protestantism. Unfortunately, what started as Luther's constructive use of anger to bring about a better church quickly deteriorated into one of the bloodiest episodes in history.

Warfare broke out in many places across Europe, pitting Christian against Christian. The largest of these wars was known as the Thirty Years' War, which lasted from 1618 until 1648 and resulted in the death of millions. Although this was essentially the last of Europe's religious wars, hostility between Protestants and Catholics has lasted for centuries in many places.

THE SALEM WITCHCRAFT TRIALS

Historians are still debating the causes of the Salem Witch-craft Trials of 1692—even today, more than 300 years after they ended. Most experts do agree that anger was responsible for at least part of the witchcraft hysteria.

In the British colony of Massachusetts during the 1600s, tensions were growing between the neighboring towns of Salem Village and Salem Town, which together were governed as one political unit. Salem Village was a farming community, while Salem Town was a port city where the people were becoming richer as their harbor thrived and trade expanded. The people of Salem Town were wealthier, worldlier, and not religious enough, as far as Salem Village was concerned. That made the villagers angry. Many of them wanted to break their ties to Salem Town and become independent, but some preferred to keep things the way they were. Anger simmered between Salem Town residents and the people of Salem Village, and also among the villagers themselves. Eventually, some of that anger would come out in accusations of witchcraft.

The first people to accuse others of being witches were Betty Parris and Abigail Williams. Betty was the nine-year-old daughter of Salem Village minister Samuel Parris, and Abigail was Samuel Parris's 12-year-old niece. Betty and Abigail and a few of their friends had been playing fortune-telling games and listening to stories about witchcraft told by Tituba, a slave owned by the Parris family. No one is sure exactly why, but the girls began to behave strangely, barking like dogs and going into trances. When no medical reason was found for their behavior, the family doctor claimed that a witch had put the girls under a spell. Eventually, the girls said Tituba and two other women from Salem Village were the ones who had bewitched them. After these three women were arrested, other people began to accuse local residents of being witches.

By the time the hysteria ended in September 1692, hundreds of people had been arrested on charges of witchcraft and 19 people—14 women and 5 men—had been executed. (Interestingly, none of the Salem "witches" was burned, as is popularly believed. The women and most of the men were hanged. One man, Giles Corey, was pressed to death with heavy stones.)

Anger was believed to be one of the signs that proved someone was a witch. If a person had publicly cursed a neighbor or displayed anger in some other way, he or she could be charged as a witch. It was easy to accuse someone of being a witch because the courts allowed "spectral evidence." That

Most historians agree that anger helped fuel the hysteria behind the infamous Salem Witchcraft Trials, depicted here in the 1853 painting, *Examination of a Witch*, by Tompkins Harrison Matteson.

means people could claim to see and hear things that were invisible to everyone else, and they could blame those visions and experiences on another person, who was then accused of being a witch. Charging a person with witchcraft was an almost foolproof way to get back at someone who had made you angry.

Anger fueled many of these accusations. As more and more people were arrested, others got even more angry and continued to make new charges, perhaps to try to get back at their neighbors, until the entire community was swirling with anger, confusion, and fear. Writer Tim Sutter explains in his 2003 article "Salem Witchcraft: The Events and Causes of the Salem Witch Trials" that the events that took place in Salem during 1692 "continue to serve as a reminder of how politics, family squabbles, religion, economics, and the imaginations and fears of people can yield tragic consequences."

THE MORMONS

In 1827, Joseph Smith of Fayette, New York, claimed that an angel had visited him and told him where to find a set of golden tablets that contained the word of God. According to Smith, the story written on the tablets described a time when Jesus Christ had come to North America and preached to the Native Americans. Smith founded the Church of Jesus Christ of Latter-day Saints, whose members were often called Mormons.

By 1843, the Mormon Church had more than 20,000 members and moved its headquarters to Illinois. As Smith's church gained followers, its members became wealthy through trade and by buying land. The Mormons' financial success made the rest of the community take notice of them. Gradually, though, people became suspicious of them, believing that they were stealing livestock and other property that belonged to local settlers. The community also grew angry over some of the Mormons' beliefs. One of the most controversial parts of Smith's religion was the idea that men could have more than one wife.

A local newspaper printed an article that criticized the fact that some Mormon men had several wives. Smith was furious at this and ordered some of his followers to destroy the newspaper's printing press. This only made the non-Mormon townspeople even angrier. They arrested Smith and his brother for the crime of vandalizing the printing press. Too

Tensions between Mormons and non-Mormons grew until Joseph Smith, founder of Mormon Church, and his brother were eventually beaten to death by an angry mob. This 1853 illustration shows Smith being tarred and feathered in an attempt to intimidate him into leaving town or renouncing his beliefs.

angry to wait for the Smith brothers to come to trial, a mob broke into the jail where they were being held and killed them in June 1844.

After Smith's death, Brigham Young led the Mormons on a trek from Illinois to Utah Territory (it was not a state at that time). There they established Salt Lake City, which remains the church's headquarters to this day. Even there, however, anger caused problems between Mormons and non-Mormon government officials. The U.S. government didn't want Young to be in charge of Utah Territory, so it sent new governor Alfred Cumming, appointed by President James Buchanan, to take Young's place. U.S. Army troops, who were prepared to fight, if necessary, followed the governor to stop any resistance from the Mormons. Although the "Mormon War" that many people expected never actually broke out, tensions remained for years between the U.S. government and the Church of Jesus Christ of Latter-day Saints.

BLEEDING KANSAS

Throughout the eighteenth century, the United States was divided by disagreements between the North and the South over the amount of power that the states and the federal government should have. The two sides were also sharply divided over whether slavery should continue to be legal. In 1854, the Kansas-Nebraska Act was passed, and it set off a wave of anger and violence that put the United States firmly on the path to Civil War.

The Kansas-Nebraska Act set up the new territories of Kansas and Nebraska. Instead of saying whether slavery would be allowed there, the act gave the people who moved there the right to vote on whether slavery would be legal or not. People from both the proslavery South and the antislavery North frantically rushed to move to Kansas so they could influence the vote on slavery. (Nebraska was far enough north that it easily became a free state that did not permit slavery.)

Fort Scott, Kansas, was the scene of one of many confrontations in the angry and violent conflict called Bleeding Kansas, a time of unrest in the 1850s between those who wanted Kansas to be a slave state and those who wanted it to be a free state.

Kansas, on the other hand, quickly became a battlefield. Angry people on both sides lashed out with violent attacks as they tried to take control of the territory. The area soon won the nickname "Bleeding Kansas."

In one particularly violent episode in May 1856, proslavery forces burned and looted the town of Lawrence, Kansas. Antislavery Northerners were furious, and a group led by abolitionist John Brown responded by attacking the town of Pottawatomie and killing five proslavery advocates. Vicious fighting raged throughout Kansas until President Franklin Pierce had to send troops to keep the peace. Kansas finally entered the Union—as a free state—in January 1861, just before the Civil War began.

THE CIVIL WAR

The Civil War between Northern and Southern states was perhaps the most destructive event in U.S. history. Bleeding Kansas was only one of many angry incidents that caused the war. As U.S. history expert Martin H. Kelly explains in his article "Top 9 Events That Led to Civil War," many factors contributed to the start of the war between the states.

One of these factors was the fury that was unleashed when the Fugitive Slave Law of 1850 was passed. This law made it a crime for federal officials *not* to arrest runaway slaves. It was intended to stop the flow of slaves who were secretly running away to the free states of the North and to Canada to escape slavery in the South. Abolitionists were enraged and they increased their efforts to help fugitive slaves—which was exactly the opposite of the law's intent.

The 1857 U.S. Supreme Court decision known as *Dred Scott* also provoked the anger of abolitionists and increased tensions between North and South. In this case, the court decided that slaves were the property of their owners, and they remained property even if they were taken into states where slavery was illegal. As a result of this controversial decision, abolitionists became even more vocal in their opposition to slavery.

Abolitionist John Brown stands out as an excellent example of how anger took control over the hearts and minds of people on both sides of the slavery issue. Brown, who had led the violent raid on Pottawatomie during the Bleeding Kansas period, let loose his rage once more in his attack on Harpers Ferry (now in West Virginia, but then a part of Virginia). On October 16, 1859, Brown and a small force of antislavery men entered the town of Harpers Ferry, intending to free the slaves living there. They hoped the attack would also launch a slave uprising that would spread throughout the South and end the fight over slavery once

(continues on page 54)

THE CANING OF SENATOR CHARLES SUMNER

The anger and violence surrounding the slavery issue during the 1850s wasn't limited to slave owners and abolitionists. In one incredible incident, it actually broke out on the floor of the U.S. Senate.

Although heated debates have always been a part of U.S. politics, what happened in May 1856 went far beyond normal behavior for politicians. Charles Sumner was a U.S. senator from Massachusetts. Despite the fact that he was a strong opponent of slavery, Sumner had not said much during the arguments over the Kansas-Nebraska Act that took place in 1854. By 1856, he was worried that the Massachusetts legislature, which had appointed him to his seat in the Senate, would not reappoint him if he didn't prove himself to be more vocal in opposing slavery. Therefore, Sumner took a stand.

On May 19, 1856, Sumner stood up in the Senate and delivered a speech called "The Crime Against Kansas." In it, he railed against the proslavery forces that had carried out violent raids in Kansas. Taking his angry words a step further, he declared that Southerners were "picked from the drunken spew and vomit of an uneasy civilization," and he claimed that fellow senator Andrew Butler (a proslavery Southerner) was a man who had taken an oath to support "the harlot [prostitute], slavery."

Perhaps understandably, Butler and many other Southerners were furious over the things Sumner had said. One of the angriest people was U.S. Congressman Preston Brooks of South Carolina, who was both a supporter of slavery and a relative of Andrew Butler. On May 22, 1856, Brooks walked into the hall of the U.S. Senate, which was not in session at the time. He went up to Sumner, who was working at his desk on the Senate floor, and began an angry confrontation. Sumner tried to get away, but his large frame was stuck inside his desk, which was bolted to the floor, and Brooks was able to strike him several times on the head with a gold-topped cane. By the time the attack was over, Sumner was lying unconscious in a pool of his own blood.

In 1856, Congressman Preston Brooks, who was angry about Senator Charles Sumner's antislavery speech and disparaging comments about the South, brutally beat Sumner with a cane on the U.S. Senate floor.

Brooks fled to avoid punishment, but his act ignited rage in both the North and the South. Supportive Southerners sent him new canes, along with messages such as "Use Knock-Down Arguments." Angry Northerners added the attack against Sumner to their list of complaints against the South.

Eventually, Brooks was forced to pay a small fine, which was his only punishment. It took Sumner years to recover fully from his injuries. He didn't return to the Senate for four years, but once he did, he became one of the most vocal opponents of the South.

(continued from page 51)

and for all. Although Army troops quickly put down Brown's revolt and sent him to be executed, the incident increased anger among both Northerners (who saw Brown as a hero who died for the cause of abolition) and Southerners (who resented Brown's attempt to control them with violence). Southerners were so angry, in fact, that they began to train local militias so they would be prepared to go to war if necessary to defend themselves against the North.

By the time Abraham Lincoln was elected president in 1860, anger was so high on both sides that Lincoln's election seemed to be the last straw. (He had not won the vote of a single Southern state.) South Carolina and, eventually, most of the slaveholding states of the country, seceded from the Union. The Civil War had begun. It would be the bloodiest war in U.S. history, leading to the deaths of more than 600,000 Americans.

RECONSTRUCTION, JIM CROW, AND THE KU KLUX KLAN

Even the North's 1865 victory over the South in the Civil War did not end the violence—or the anger—that had started the war. In fact, it seemed as if angry feelings on both sides actually increased after the war. The period following the war, when the Southern states were slowly brought back into the Union, was known as Reconstruction.

Most of the battles of the Civil War had been fought on Southern territory. Because of this, the South and its cities, farms, and economy were all in ruins by the end of the war. The Southern people, too, were left feeling angry and resentful, and they feared what would happen to them as the victorious North set about to put the nation back together. Most of all, Southerners were furious that the North expected them to accept the freedom of the former slaves and to treat them as equals under the law.

The South didn't have the power to control the laws the North was passing to benefit former slaves, so angry Southerners did whatever they could to make sure that a strict separation between whites and blacks remained in force. Historian Walter Lynwood Fleming described the intense anger that Southern whites were experiencing during Reconstruction; he explained that blacks, with their newly won rights, "were everywhere considered offensive by the native whites. . . . [The freed black person] was more than Southern temper could tranquilly bear, and race conflicts were frequent."

Since the political influence of white Southerners was limited, they often channeled their anger into private organizations rather than official political parties. Southerners banded together to form groups such as the Ku Klux Klan, which used violence and terror to prevent blacks from exercising their freedoms and their political and economic rights.

Over time, Southerners gained back some of their political power. As they won back some control over local and state legislatures, the former Confederates once again channeled their anger into politics. They put Black Codes, or Jim Crow laws, into effect, which set up a system of strict segregation between blacks and whites in almost all public places. This included everything from trains and restaurants to which water fountains people could use to get a quick drink. The separation of the races would last through the mid-twentieth century, ending only with the success of the civil rights movement of the 1950s and 1960s.

THE HOLOCAUST

The Holocaust is the name given to Nazi Germany's attempt to rid the world of Jews. By the time the Holocaust ended in 1945, the Nazis had succeeded in killing about 6 million European Jews, along with millions of other people such as Poles, Serbs, and Gypsies. The Holocaust may be history's most extreme example of how destructive anger can be.

Anti-Semitism, or hatred of Jews, was not something new that began when the Nazis came to power in Germany under Adolf Hitler in 1933. In fact, anti-Semitism had existed in Europe for centuries. European Christians had long viewed Jews as being on the edge of society. Some Christians even believed that the Jews had killed Jesus Christ, though he was actually executed by the Romans. Partly because of this, the Jewish community was often blamed for various problems, including epidemics of plague. Jews were also accused of poisoning water wells and killing Christian children. In the sixteenth century, Protestant leader Martin Luther said that Jewish people were unfit to live. Centuries later, Adolf Hitler

German Chancellor Adolf Hitler makes a speech in May of 1933 in Berlin. Hitler focused his anger on the Jews as he tried to encourage Germans to blame their problems after World War I on people of that faith.

and the Nazi Party continued this long tradition of hatred and attacks against Jews.

After the Germans lost to the Allies in World War I (1914–1918), Germany was left humiliated and in ruins, much like the Southern states after the U.S. Civil War. As part of the peace treaty that ended the war, Germany was forced to pay the Allies huge amounts of money as punishment for having started the war. Germany sunk into a crisis because of these payments, along with economic troubles that were troubling the entire world during the 1920s and 1930s. Money became almost worthless. In some cases, people had to push wheelbarrows full of paper money to the market just to buy a loaf of bread.

These terrible economic conditions left the German people angry and frustrated, and desperate to find a way back to the prosperity they had enjoyed before the war. Hitler took advantage of the people's desperation and gave them the perfect scapegoat to blame for their problems: the Jews. According to Hitler, it was the Jews who were responsible for Germany's defeat in World War I and for the financial troubles that the Germans faced after the war. By getting rid of the Jews, Hitler said, Germany would be able to return to a position of power and influence on the world stage.

Hitler's plan worked. Many Germans developed intense anger toward Jews, and went along willingly as the Nazis passed laws aimed at taking away Jewish people's rights. Eventually, the Nazis' plans included eliminating Jews from society altogether. The murder of two-thirds of the Jewish population of Europe during the Holocaust stands out as a terrifying reminder of just how destructive anger can be.

CONSTRUCTIVE USES OF ANGER IN HISTORY

The world needs anger. The world often continues to allow evil because it isn't angry enough.

—Bede Jarrett (1881–1937), English priest

Anger isn't always a bad thing. In fact, when it is expressed properly and channeled toward a worthwhile cause, it can have positive effects. Anger tends to have a bad reputation because, as was previously discussed, it is often accompanied by violence. Yet, anger can be a very useful tool. As psychologist and anger management expert Dr. Lyle Becourtney writes in the 2007 article "Anger Can Be Positive":

Outraged by the mistreatment of others, many have pushed for new laws over the years, including those to protect children, the mentally ill and mentally challenged, people of different religious and ethnic backgrounds, the handicapped and disabled, and many other groups. Countless people have been helped by the actions of those who experienced anger and decided to do something positive to make things better.

In many situations, it is hard to imagine that change could ever take place without anger. In the March 2003 issue of the *APA Monitor on Psychology*, social psychologist Carol Tarvis is quoted as saying, "Imagine what the women's suffrage movement would have been like if women had said, 'Guys, it's really so unfair; we're nice people and we're human beings, too. Won't you listen to us and give us the vote?'" If women had remained polite and held back the anger they felt at being treated as second-class citizens, the women's rights movement might never have come about, much less succeeded.

Constructive anger is especially useful when a lot of people get angry at the same thing. "The same issues that can arouse anger in individuals can also arouse anger in large groups," explains University of Colorado political scientist Phil Barker. When this happens, the anger becomes something called "social rage"—and social rage has been the driving force behind some of the greatest social movements in history, from the abolition of slavery to the women's rights movement. Let's explore some of the best uses of constructive anger and social rage in history.

THE AMERICAN REVOLUTION

When Great Britain first began to create colonies in North America in the early seventeenth century, no one could have imagined that one day the settlers would rebel against their mother country and start a new nation of their own. In fact, if the colonists hadn't become intensely angry at the way they were being treated by the British government, there might never have been an American Revolution or a United States of America.

The trouble began after the British fought the French for control of the territory around the Appalachian Mountains, Mississippi River, and parts of Canada in the French and

Angry about how they were being treated by British rulers, American colonists rebelled and fought for their freedom in the Revolutionary War. In this illustration, Americans in New York City tear down a statue of England's King George III in 1776 as a celebration of their independence.

Indian War of 1754 to 1763. Although the British won the war and took over the land, the war had been very expensive. England was left with a huge amount of debt to pay. To help with some of that cost, the British government turned to their North American colonies. By increasing taxes on the colonists, England planned to make enough money to pay off its war debt.

Before this time, the colonists had enjoyed a lot of freedom. They paid few taxes and had their own local governments. In fact, sometimes it seemed as if the British were hardly paying any attention to the colonies at all. When England suddenly began to impose new taxes, the colonists were furious. Each new tax—such as the Stamp Act and the Tea Act—made the colonists angrier. They declared that they shouldn't have to pay taxes to the British government since they didn't have representatives to defend their interests in the British Parliament. The situation became even more heated when King George III took away the colonies' right to govern themselves. After all the years they had been ignored by England, the colonists were enraged. They believed the king was treating them like disobedient children.

By 1775, the colonists were angry enough to engage in battle against the British. After the Declaration of Independence was issued in 1776, the colonies became the United States of America. Although the war raged on until 1781, the former colonists were able to take the anger they felt over their mistreatment by the British and channel it into the creation of a new democratic government. Although the United States began in its history with the bloodshed of war, it ultimately prevented future violence by creating a system in which political power could be transferred from one president and one Congress to the next without the revolts and civil wars that often took place in other countries. And, because other nations were inspired by the American Revolution to adopt similar political systems, countless other civil wars may have been prevented.

THE ABOLITION MOVEMENT

Although slavery was legal for a time in the United States, there were sharp differences in opinion between the North and the South over whether the brutal practice should continue. Seeing the terrible lives the slaves were forced to lead and the harsh ways in which many slave owners treated their slaves made some people very angry. Their social rage ignited a new movement—abolitionism—that would eventually bring about the end of slavery in the United States.

Even in the Southern states, where slavery was viewed as essential to the economy, there were many people who were frustrated about the treatment of slaves. Because slaves were considered property, not people, they could be bought or sold at any time, and they could be separated from their families without even being able to say goodbye. Many slaves were housed in crowded shacks, most were forced to perform difficult manual labor from sunrise to sunset, and some were beaten if they didn't work fast enough or if they didn't live up to their owners' expectations.

Some Southerners—including George Washington, Thomas Jefferson, and Patrick Henry—spoke out against slavery. Despite the fact that he owned slaves himself, Jefferson hoped to find a way to end the institution of slavery. He wrote, "Nobody wishes more ardently [than I do] to see an abolition, not only of the trade, but of the condition of slavery; and certainly, nobody will be more willing to encounter every sacrifice for that object."

It would take a few other events to stir up enough anger for people to finally take on slavery and destroy it. One of those events happened in 1850, with the passage of the Fugitive Slave Law. This law stated that all people—whether they lived in the North or the South—were required to help catch and return runaway slaves to their owners. Furious

Northerners saw the law as a license for Southern slave owners to kidnap former slaves who had escaped to freedom in the North. To try to counteract the effects of the law, many Northern states passed "personal liberty" laws, which said that state judges would not be allowed to help return

Harriet Beecher Stowe's 1852 novel, *Uncle Tom's Cabin*, helped fuel readers' anger about slavery and encouraged them to join the abolitionist movement.

slaves to their owners. Northerners became even angrier when the U.S. Supreme Court decided that these state laws were invalid because the federal Fugitive Slave Law overruled state laws.

One woman was particularly angry about the Fugitive Slave Law. Her name was Harriet Beecher Stowe, and the novel she published in 1852, *Uncle Tom's Cabin*, brought a new sense of urgency to the abolition movement. The book was about a hardworking slave named Tom who was brutally abused by a cruel master. Stowe's powerful depiction of the terrible conditions under which slaves lived riled up Northerners. Even people who had not been active in the abolition movement before became angry enough to join the fight against slavery.

It would ultimately take the Civil War to overturn the institution of slavery for good. Even so, the abolition movement was powerful, and one of the most effective uses of social rage in U.S. history.

THOMAS EDISON: MAKING FRUSTRATION YOUR FRIEND

Few things are as frustrating as trying hard to do something and failing over and over again. When things just don't seem to be working, it's easy to give up. Sometimes, though, the frustration you feel can actually help keep you going until you finally achieve success.

It worked for Thomas Edison, the inventor of the phonograph, the movie camera, and the lightbulb. Edison spent years and failed literally thousands of times before he finally succeeded in making his lightbulb work. Despite all his failures, Edison never let his frustration get the better of him. "If I find 10,000 ways something won't work, I haven't failed," he explained. "I am not discouraged because every wrong attempt discarded is just one more step forward."

THE WOMEN'S SUFFRAGE MOVEMENT

In 1840, the World's Anti-slavery Convention was held in London. Abolitionists from all over the world—most of them men—attended the event. There were a few women at the convention, but instead of letting them sit with the rest of the delegates, the organizers of the convention made them sit behind a curtain while speeches were being made. They also wouldn't allow the women to make any speeches of their own. Two of the women—Americans Elizabeth Cady Stanton and Lucretia Mott—were enraged at the way the male delegates treated them. As the National Women's History Museum explains on its

Productive anger led Elizabeth Cady Stanton (pictured here with her daughter, Harriot, in 1856) and Lucretia Mott to hold the Seneca Falls Convention in 1848. There, they publicly expressed their concerns about the unfair treatment of women and helped kick-start the women's movement.

Web site, "Stanton and Mott, like other activist women in the United States, began to see similarities between their own . . . status and that of the slaves."

Their anger inspired them to hold a convention of their own at Seneca Falls, New York, in 1848. At the convention they publicly expressed their frustration with the way women were treated in the United States. They called for a series of changes that would improve women's position in society, giving women the right to hold property, divorce their husbands, and vote, the latter of which is called suffrage.

After the Seneca Falls Convention, the women's movement was in high gear. Angry women engaged in many forms of protest to try to demonstrate that they deserved the same rights that men enjoyed. Over the years, suffrage leaders became more and more outspoken and militant, and the tactics they used got more and more controversial. In 1872, suffragist Susan B. Anthony voted in a local election, ignoring the protests of polling officials. She was arrested, but she inspired many other women to attempt to vote, too. That same year, Victoria Woodhull declared herself a candidate for president of the United States, despite the fact that she didn't even have the right to vote for herself in the election.

The fight for women's right to vote would last until 1920, when the Nineteenth Amendment to the Constitution was finally ratified, and women's suffrage became a reality. The suffrage movement did more than just win women the right to vote. As the National Women's History Museum notes, "women generated their own style of politics—beginning with the drive for woman suffrage—organizing at the grassroots level around major political and social issues. . . . [Women] helped to shape much of twentieth century social policy." And it all started because two women became angry.

RESISTANCE TO THE NAZIS

The Holocaust brought about the deaths of some 6 million Jews during World War II. The fact that two-thirds of Europe's Jewish population died may lead some people to believe that no one opposed the Nazis as they carried out the brutal work of getting rid of an entire group of people. There were also, however, many people who resisted the Nazis—despite the dangers they faced doing so—because of their anger at the way the Nazis were treating the Jews and other

HELEN KELLER OVERCOMES FRUSTRATION AND ANGER

When Helen Keller was born in Alabama in 1880, she was a healthy child. Yet, 18 months later, tragedy struck. Helen caught a serious fever. Although she survived the illness, she was left blind, deaf, and unable to speak. She was a smart child, but her inability to communicate with her family filled her with frustration and anger. Helen had temper tantrums, broke dishes, and threw lamps, and she displayed terrible table manners, refusing to use a fork and often grabbing food off other people's plates. Her family didn't know what to do and considered sending Helen to a mental institution.

Everything changed after Annie Sullivan, a 20-year-old graduate of the Perkins School for the Blind, came to be Helen's teacher in 1887. Sullivan was able to break through to Helen, teaching her words by spelling them with her fingers on the palm of Helen's hand. The Keller family was amazed at the change in Helen. Under Sullivan's guidance, Helen was able to transfer all the anger that had built up inside her toward learning new things. She not only learned to communicate; she also became the first blind and deaf person to graduate from college and she went on to write 11 books and countless articles.

ethnic groups. From sabotaging the Nazi military to leading uprisings, the resistance took many forms. One of the most dangerous ways to resist Nazi Germany was to hide Jewish people so they could not be rounded up and sent to concentration camps.

Adolf Hitler did his best to direct the German people's anger toward Jews as he rose to power. Still, not everyone bought into Hitler's claims that Jewish people were responsible for Germany's financial problems after World War I. Many people worked with Jews or had Jewish friends. When the Nazis began to force Jews to live in crowded ghettos and to wear yellow stars on their clothing to indicate that they were Jewish, some non-Jewish people were outraged. Some were so angry that they decided to risk their own lives to try to protect their Jewish friends.

The story of Anne Frank and her family is probably the best-known example of non-Jews hiding their Jewish friends. The Franks were a Jewish family of four living in Holland when Nazi Germany began to invade other nations in Europe. In 1942, Anne's father, Otto Frank, asked for the help of four non-Jewish friends: Miep Gies, Victor Kugler, Johannes Kleiman, and Bep Voskuijl. Otto Frank's four friends were all frustrated with the terrible treatment the Jews were receiving

Otto Frank (*center*) and his family were helped by (*from left*) Miep Gies, Johannes Kleiman, Victor Kugler, and Bep Voskuijl, who were angered by the way the Nazis were treating Jewish people. Gies had been Otto's secretary and later guarded Anne Frank's diary, which is now one of the world's most read books.

at the hands of the Nazis, and they were ready to do whatever they could to oppose the Nazi regime. As Otto Frank explained in a letter he wrote after the war was over, "All four [of the people who helped hide the Franks] immediately agreed, though they were fully aware of the dangerous task they would be taking upon themselves in doing so. By Nazi law, everyone helping Jews was severely punished and risked being put into prison, being deported or even shot."

With the help of their friends, the Franks left their home and moved into the attic of an office building. They remained there in hiding until the Nazis discovered them in 1944. Anne, her parents, and her sister were arrested and sent to concentration camps. Otto Frank was the only member of the family to survive. The attempt to save the Franks was just one example of ordinary people's efforts to channel their anger at the Nazis into useful forms of resistance.

THE STRUGGLE TO END APARTHEID

European countries began to claim parts of Africa as colonies for themselves beginning as early as the seventeenth century and lasting through the nineteenth century. Many African territories remained under the control of European nations until well into the twentieth century. Among the European holdings in Africa was South Africa, where eventually the European government put laws into place that limited the rights of black Africans and put the white minority firmly in charge of the country. This system of segregation and discrimination in South Africa was known as apartheid.

Although black South Africans never approved of apartheid, it was not until the middle of the twentieth century that an organized opposition to the system began to form. Among the groups that worked to overturn apartheid was the African National Congress (ANC). Its members included activists such as Walter Sisulu, Oliver Tambo, and Nelson Mandela. They organized strikes, boycotts, and other demonstrations to show their anger over unfair policies, such

Former ANC Secretary-General Walter Sisulu speaks to students in 1990 in South Africa, where he had met with local leaders about ending political fights in Natal. The ANC and leaders like Sisulu turned their anger about apartheid into productive, nonviolent activism against the unfair policies.

as the government's requirement that black South Africans carry a special identification pass whenever they went out in public.

Unfortunately, though, not all opponents of apartheid limited their activities to nonviolent protests. Some committed violent acts, such as bombings, that were intended to terrorize the government and force it to end apartheid.

Many antiapartheid activists were put on trial for their participation in protests against the government. One of these activists was Mandela, who had become one of the movement's most vocal leaders. Mandela was found guilty of treason and sentenced to life in prison. For 27 years, he carried on his struggle against apartheid despite the fact that he remained in prison. As a result, he became a symbol of the antiapartheid movement.

Throughout the 1970s and 1980s, the rest of the world began to take notice of what was going on in South Africa. Other countries expressed their anger over the way blacks were being treated, and it became harder and harder for South Africa's white-led government to keep their system of apartheid. International companies pulled out of South Africa to show their support for the antiapartheid movement.

Eventually, the economic problems caused by fleeing corporations made South Africa reconsider apartheid. In 1986, South African President Pieter Willem Botha said publicly that South Africa had "outgrown the outdated concept of apartheid." By 1990, the government was actively removing the laws that had held apartheid in place. Mandela was released from prison in February 1990, and on May 9, 1994, he was elected president of South Africa. On that day, it was clear that the movement to end apartheid had succeeded.

GANDHI AND NONVIOLENCE

Mohandas Karamchand Gandhi, better known as Mahatma Gandhi, led the struggle to end Great Britain's rule of India. He may be history's best-known example of someone who knew how to use his anger peacefully to achieve goals. Born in Porbandar, India, in 1869, Gandhi became a lawyer and got a job in South Africa, where the system of apartheid was in full force. Apartheid didn't just discriminate against black South Africans. Anyone who wasn't white was affected by the system, and so, as an Indian, Gandhi was affected.

His anger was sparked one day in 1893, when he was riding in the first-class car of a train. Even though he had

Gandhi is photographed in his time as a young lawyer circa 1906. He inspired future leaders, such as like Martin Luther King Jr. and Nelson Mandela, to use anger peacefully with nonviolent protest.

a first-class ticket, a white official told Gandhi that he had to move to the third-class car. When Gandhi refused, the official threw him and all of his belongings off the train. Gandhi was so furious at the way he had been treated that he vowed to devote himself to fighting racial inequality wherever it might exist. He spent years in South Africa doing just that: publishing articles and organizing protests to oppose the system of apartheid. As part of his struggle, he developed a philosophy of the best way to fight injustice. It was called *satyagraha*, which translates to "holding on to truth." Simply put, it meant opposing injustice with nonviolent methods.

In 1915, Gandhi went home to India, where he put his anger—and his belief in nonviolence—to work once again. This time it was to oppose British rule over his native country. His insistence on nonviolence won him respect around the world, and by 1947, the British had agreed to withdraw from India. The nation became independent on August 15, 1947.

Gandhi knew that anger was at the heart of his success. He wrote, "I have learned through bitter experience the one supreme lesson to conserve my anger, and as heat conserved is transmuted [changed] into energy, even so our anger controlled can be transmuted into a power which can move the world."

In a speech at the Santa Monica Community Center in 1998, Gandhi's grandson Arun Gandhi described what his grandfather had taught him about anger. "Gandhi taught that anger was a very good thing if understood and channeled effectively and intelligently," Arun said. "He said anger was like electricity, which if abused can destroy us all. But, if channeled intelligently, can be used for the good of all society."

THE CIVIL RIGHTS MOVEMENT

The civil rights movement of the 1950s and 1960s in the United States was a response to the decades of unequal treatment blacks had faced since the Civil War ended slavery. Although blacks were free, they did not enjoy the same rights as white Americans. This was especially true in the South, where Jim Crow laws kept the races separated and violent groups, such as the Ku Klux Klan, terrorized black Americans.

Perhaps the best-known leader of the civil rights movement was Dr. Martin Luther King Jr. He used Gandhi's same nonviolent tactics and shared his belief in using anger to bring about positive change. Born in 1929 in Atlanta, Georgia, King's experiences as a young man helped spark his anger at the way blacks were treated in the United States. When he was in high school, he was traveling home from a school trip on a bus. As white people boarded the bus, the driver told King and his teacher that they had to stand and move to the back of the bus to make room for the white passengers to sit. Although he refused at first, King eventually gave in and moved. He never forgot how he felt in that moment. "That night will never leave my mind," he later wrote. "It was the angriest I have ever been in my life."

Years later, as he organized protests against segregation and helped lead the fight to win equal rights for African Americans, King continued to use his anger as fuel to keep his struggle going. He kept working even at times when it seemed like the movement would never succeed. Despite his anger, he always remembered the importance of non-violence—especially when he and other civil rights activists faced violence at the hands of police and other pro-segregation forces. King wrote, "Returning violence for violence multiplies violence. . . . Hate cannot drive out hate. Only love can do that."

As Georgetown University sociology professor Michael Eric Dyson explains, "What united King . . . is the incurable love that fueled his hopefulness and rage. As King's example proves, as we dream, we must remember the poor and vulnerable who live a nightmare. And as we strike out in . . . anger against injustice, love must cushion even our hardest blows." King's anger—and his insistence on cushioning that rage with love and nonviolence—helped turn society upside down and brought about equal rights for all Americans.

FRUSTRATION AND ANGER TODAY

He is a fool who cannot be angry; but he is a wise man who will not.

—*Seneca (c. 54 B.C.–A.D. 39),
Roman philosopher*

In today's society, we are all too familiar with the destructive side of anger. "The abortion clinic bombers and schoolhouse shooters of recent decades may be the most violent examples of contemporary American rage," writes journalist Andrew Santella in his 2007 article, "All the Rage." However, he continues, "don't forget strident bloggers, finger-pointing cable-news hosts, brawling professional athletes, bullying grade-schoolers, and those Little League parents who go after umpires, veins bulging."

Although destructive anger is common, it's important to remember that there are also large numbers of people who use their anger in constructive ways to try to make the world better.

DESTRUCTIVE USES OF ANGER
Terrorism

The use of terrorist tactics, such as suicide bombings, has become something that people live with every day in certain parts of the world, particularly in the Middle East. When airline hijackers attacked the United States on September 11, 2001, they brought terrorism much closer to home for most Americans.

Since that day, anger—often, very destructive anger—has become common both among terrorists and among Americans and their antiterrorism allies. For years, researchers have been trying to figure out what leads people to commit terrorist acts. Perhaps it isn't surprising that one of the main reasons people become terrorists is their anger.

When it comes to radical Islamic terrorists like those who carried out the September 11, 2001 attacks, the anger is the result of a few different factors. For one, as British writer Bill Johnson explains, "The attitude of many Muslims towards the West and Christianity is colored by the Crusades of medieval times and European domination and colonialism." Religious conflict expert Austin Cline says, "The image of barbaric Christian Crusaders continues to haunt Arab Muslim perspectives of Europe and Christianity." The United States is actively involved in the Middle East, supporting Israel and (after the 2001 attacks) fighting battles in Iraq and Afghanistan. This fact has led to deep frustration among many people who were already angry for other reasons.

Many terrorist recruits are young men who believe the world is unfair. While they live in poverty, they see the United States and other nations becoming richer and more powerful. In the eyes of these young people, their lands and, especially, their Islamic faith, are threatened by the strength of countries such as the United States. Bill Johnson explains that the messages of terrorist leaders like Osama bin Laden "find receptive ears because over three centuries, the Muslim world has fallen behind the West politically, economically, and militarily."

When young, idealistic Muslims see the United States playing an active role in the Middle East, they become angry and frustrated. They often feel helpless, as if there is nothing they can do to protect their civilization from outside influence. They begin to look for ways to overcome their feelings of frustration. Plus, as journalist David Ignatius writes in the *Washington Post*, "Muslim terrorists thrive by channeling and perverting the idealism of young people." According to divinity student Andrew Lumpkin, the violence of terrorism becomes "an act of symbolic empowerment: groups who believe they are victims of oppression use violence to show others their power and self-worth." Their frustration and anger become so strong that they begin to see terrorism as a reasonable outlet for expressing their rage.

The terrorists aren't the only ones who are angry. In the wake of the 2001 attacks, in addition to fear and anxiety, most Americans felt intense anger over what had happened. Auburn University professor Roderick T. Long explains the role anger played after the attacks: "Our anger gives form to our moral perception, putting us in . . . contact with two ethical facts: the wrongness of the attack, and the rightness of retaliating against it. To that extent, our anger sharpens our vision. . . . However, anger too can be an overeager servant, prompting us to act in ways that may not square with the very facts of reason to which our anger is being responsive."

In the months after the 2001 attacks, the United States began what government officials and the media called the War on Terror, launching an attack against Afghanistan and, in 2003, Iraq. Some observers have argued that the rapid U.S. military response after the terrorist attacks was carried out in anger and was not planned well enough to ensure that the mission would be successful. As Long writes:

Our anger embodies a judgment that what the terrorists did on September 11th was wrong. . . . If, in the anger of our military response, we are heedless of the lives of innocent civilians in Afghanistan or elsewhere, then, in the name of our anger, we will have infringed the very principle that our anger is supposed to be expressing: We [rather than the terrorists] will be the ones raining down death from the skies upon innocent civilians in order to express a grievance against their government.

In other words, our anger, too, may be destructive.

Ecoterrorists and Animal Rights Activists

Americans have a long history of using their anger to bring about changes in society. Although many of these movements—such as abolition and the civil rights movements—emphasized nonviolence, not all groups of angry activists believe they can get what they want without committing a few acts of destruction.

Among the most visible of these groups are people called ecoterrorists, who destroy property and injure other people in their attempt to protect the environment or the rights of animals. In recent years, ecoterrorists haven't even bothered to hide the fact that they have come to believe violence is necessary to achieve their goals. In 2002, for example, the radical environmental group Earth Liberation Front (ELF) claimed responsibility for a fire that had been set at the U.S. Forest Service research station in Irvine, Pennsylvania. Along with the statement in which the group admitted to starting the fire, ELF also issued a warning that said, "[W]here it is necessary, we will no longer hesitate to pick up the gun to implement justice."

Many of the people who are committed to saving animals and the environment harbor deep anger over the way human beings have treated Earth and the living things on it. People for the Ethical Treatment of Animals (PETA) may be

Ingrid Newkirk channeled her frustration over cruelty to animals into the creation of PETA. Seen here in 1998, Newkirk sits in a cage in Taipei, Taiwan, during a protest of what she said is the abusive trading of pets there.

the best-known pro-animal rights group. According to the group's Web site, PETA believes "that animals are not ours to eat, wear, experiment on, or use for entertainment."

PETA was founded in 1980 by Ingrid Newkirk. She traces her own rage over the poor treatment of animals to an incident she witnessed at the age of eight. On a trip to India, she witnessed a man beating a bull in the street. She later said, "I was filled with so much anger and panic to stop this man." That anger eventually led her to start PETA and engage in controversial demonstrations, such as splashing fake blood on people who wear fur coats and breaking into shops that sell fur. Although many people view PETA's activities as excessive, most agree that PETA is nowhere near as destructive as another animal rights group, the Animal Liberation Front (ALF).

ALF is not an official nonprofit group like PETA. Instead, it is a secret organization whose members carry out attacks on laboratories that perform testing on animals. ALF members set the lab animals free and sometimes destroy valuable equipment or even burn down buildings. Radical British animal rights activist Keith Mann described ALF's activities: "Labs raided, locks glued, products spiked, depots ransacked, windows smashed, construction halted, mink set free, fences torn down, cabs burnt out, offices in flames, car tires slashed, cages emptied, phone lines severed, . . . hunt dogs stolen, fur coats slashed, buildings destroyed, foxes freed, kennels attacked, businesses burgled, uproar, anger, outrage. . . . It's an ALF thing!"

Most destructive animal rights activists continue to insist that they only destroy property and would never harm people physically. There are others, however, who are so angry that they have stated publicly that they wouldn't rule out murder as a way to stop the abuse of animals. Jerry Vlasak, a California surgeon, spoke at a 2003 animal rights conference. "I don't think you'd have to kill—assassinate—too many vivisectors [people who experiment on animals] before you would see a marked decrease in the amount of vivisection going on," he said. "And I think for 5 lives, 10 lives, 15 human lives, we could save a million, 2 million, 10 million nonhuman animals."

School Shootings

School shootings that have taken place in recent years—for example, at Columbine High School in Colorado in 1999 and at Virginia Tech in 2007—have led researchers to study the reasons why certain students choose to commit violent acts that harm or even kill their peers and teachers. Perhaps not surprisingly, almost all of the studies that have been done have shown that anger is the main motivation behind school shootings.

An August 2007 study conducted by the Shyness Research Institute in Indiana examined the sad circumstances of school shootings. The staff of the American Psychological Association and World Science wrote that the study "claims to offer answers for why most . . . school massacres occur: students rejected by peers withdraw, [and] then get angry and lash out."

Bullying was one of the biggest factors that determined whether a student would become angry enough to commit a violent attack. As writer Sandra P. Thomas explains in her 2004 article, "School Connectedness, Anger Behaviors, and Relationships of Violent and Nonviolent American Youth," kids who became school shooters "were social outcasts who had experienced bullying and other forms of cruel treatment from classmates." In 2001, the National Threat Assessment Center studied 37 school shootings and reported that in two-thirds of the incidents, the shooters said that they had felt "persecuted, bullied, threatened, attacked, or injured." Thomas went on to explain that "teasing and bullying escalated when students were highly sensitive, cried, or acted 'odd.'"

Although being bullied would make anyone angry, the way a person responds to his or her anger ultimately determines how the person acts. Few schools provide education and training on how to manage anger and turn it into positive energy. Because of this, it is all too common for students to turn to violence when they express their angry feelings. "While some students react to harassment and bullying by staying home from school or withdrawing from peers, others retaliate with fists or weapons," Thomas says. To stop school shootings, it is essential to stop bullying and to learn how to deal with anger. In many cases, students who are at risk can get the help they need before they go down a violent path.

ROAD RAGE

Getting angry while driving a car, called road rage, is one of the most common and most dangerous types of anger in modern society. As previously discussed, a person's body goes through some possibly unhealthy changes when he or she gets angry. For example, blood pressure rises and the heart beats faster. Going through these kinds of changes while driving is even more dangerous because intense anger can easily make someone lose control of the car and cause an accident.

The AAA Foundation for Traffic Safety did a study of car accidents that took place between 1990 and 1996. According to the study, in those six years alone, road rage was responsible for 218 deaths and more than 12,000 injuries. What's even scarier than these figures is that the study also found that road rage incidents are increasing by 5 to 10 percent every year.

Anything that happens while driving can send someone into a rage if he or she is not prepared to handle it. Annoyances that could result in road rage include another driver going too slowly, someone driving too close to another car, someone cutting in front of a line of waiting cars, and countless other driving situations. Drivers who experience road rage may pound their fists on the steering wheel, shout at other drivers, or flash obscene gestures. Expressing their anger makes them feel more powerful, at least for a while. It may make them feel as though they have some control over the frustrating things that other drivers are doing. But, as anger management experts Glenn Schiraldi and Melissa Hallmark Kerr point out, "road rage is no more effective in the long run than any other form of problem anger. And it might be more dangerous."

There are many different techniques that can help cool road rage. Even something as simple as loosening one's grip on the steering wheel can make a person feel more relaxed and less likely to lash out in anger.

Vigilantes

A vigilante is someone who takes the law into his or her own hands in an attempt to bring about justice—at least, justice as the vigilante sees it. In the nineteenth century, vigilantes attacked new immigrants such as the Irish and Chinese because they were angry about the fact that the newcomers were taking jobs that might have gone to other Americans. "Almost every decade, some sinister group of self-proclaimed patriots mobilizes to repel a new invasion from some . . . threat or other. Their wrath has almost always been directed against the poorest, most powerless, and hardest-working segment of the population: recent migrants," writes author Mike Davis in his 2005 article "Vigilante Man."

One of the most famous groups of vigilantes are the Minutemen, a group of armed men who patrol the border between Arizona and Mexico, trying to prevent Mexicans from crossing into the United States illegally. As Davis explains, they have "harassed, illegally detained, beaten, and possibly murdered immigrants crossing through the desert... of Arizona and California." Rather than using the systems of justice and politics to control immigration, these kinds of vigilantes channel their anger into acts that can be both illegal and violent.

CONSTRUCTIVE USES OF ANGER
The Story of Kevin Everett

On September 9, 2007, Buffalo Bills football player Kevin Everett suffered a severe spinal injury during the kickoff of the second half of a game. When he went to tackle Denver Broncos player Domenik Hixon, Everett dislocated his neck, which made his bones pinch his spinal cord. He was rushed to the hospital, where doctors declared that the injury was "catastrophic." They said that Everett would probably never walk again.

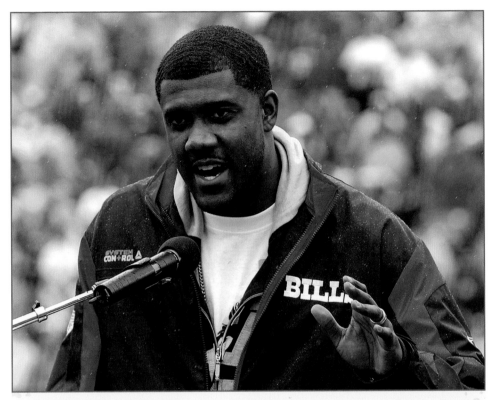

Former Buffalo Bills tight end Kevin Everett, seen here speaking to football fans in 2008, directed his sadness and anger toward learning to walk again after doctors told him his football injury would likely leave him unable to do so.

At first, Everett was saddened and discouraged by the news. "The first couple of weeks he would sit in darkness in his hospital bedroom," said Rafferty Laredo, a medical specialist who worked to help Everett get better. "I think it was extremely discouraging for him to know what he was like before and at this point not able to do anything."

Everett didn't let his anger and sadness keep him down. He became determined to regain the use of his body. The first weeks and months after the injury were full of frustration as Everett tried and failed to move the way he used to before he was hurt. Still, he remained positive and channeled his anger toward the goal of walking again. Amazingly, less than five months after the accident, Everett took his first steps on his own. He had succeeded at something that seemed impossible. As his mother, Patricia Dugas, put it, "He's a tiger, you know, he's strong. . . . [T]hey can't tell Kevin what he can't do."

Managing Anger in Exile: The Dalai Lama

The Dalai Lama is the title given to the leader of Tibet, an area in Asia that was once an independent country but has been occupied by China since 1959. Tenzin Gyatso, the current Dalai Lama, has been in exile ever since he had to flee from Chinese forces as they took over Tibet. He has been living in India and traveling around the world since that time. For decades, he has spoken out against the Chinese occupation, hoping that Tibet will be a free and independent nation again someday. Despite his anger at China, the Dalai Lama has always insisted that violence should not be used to try to free Tibet. Managing his anger is one of the main goals of the Dalai Lama's life and of his Buddhist religious practice.

Events in Tibet in 2008 forced the Dalai Lama to address the issue of nonviolence and anger control even more than he normally does. In June of that year, protesters in favor of freeing Tibet from China held violent demonstrations. This led the Chinese authorities to respond with violence to stop the protests. The Dalai Lama has said that he respects the passion of these young protesters, but he still believes that nonviolence is the best strategy. He has often shared his own struggles with anger.

In an article written by Howard C. Cutler in *Psychology Today*, the Dalai Lama explains how to handle anger: "[L]et's say that someone does you harm. Your immediate response

The fourteenth Dalai Lama (*left*) greets China's former communist leader Mao Tse-Tung in 1954. At the time, the Dalai Lama was promised that Tibet's autonomy from China would come in time and he was quoted as thanking the communist leaders of China for reconstruction work in Tibet, which had been invaded by Chinese troops in 1950. In March of 2009, the Dalai Lama—frustrated by Chinese leaders' actions—spoke out about China's rule of Tibet, but promised to continue to work with leaders to improve relations.

might be to become angry, but then you reflect upon the destructive nature of anger, and that immediately makes you more cautious of giving in to the anger and letting it escalate." The Dalai Lama makes clear his belief that the people who make you angry aren't really your enemy. As he is quoted in the book, *The Pocket Dalai Lama*, "Anger is the real destroyer of our good human qualities; an enemy with a weapon cannot destroy these qualities, but anger can. Anger is our real enemy."

Nonviolent Environmental Groups

As described earlier, ecoterrorists are people who are so angry over the state of the environment that they engage in violence in order to make their voices heard. Other environmental activists are just as angry and frustrated, but they channel their anger into nonviolent demonstrations that win the respect and support of people and governments.

One of the best-known environmental organizations is Greenpeace. Founded in 1971, this group has worked to stop nuclear testing, whaling, deforestation, and global warming. They do not do this by destroying research facilities or businesses that hurt the environment. Instead, the members of Greenpeace carry out demonstrations in which only they themselves are at risk of injury. For example, they might sail their boats in the way of passing whaling ships. The group also uses more political methods, such as working to persuade politicians to pass laws to help the environment. Greenpeace also holds conferences to explain its beliefs to the public.

The Sierra Club is another nonviolent environmental organization. It was started in 1892, making it the oldest environmental group in the United States. Like Greenpeace, the Sierra Club uses techniques such as public education to help save the environment. The group plainly declares that Sierra Club members do not use violence or destruction to demonstrate their position. According to the group's mission statement, in its effort to "Explore, enjoy, and protect the wild places of the Earth," it will "use all lawful means to carry out these objectives."

After a repeat drunk driving offender hit and killed her young daughter, Candy Lightner was angry enough to create the organization Mothers Against Drunk Driving (MADD). Here, she speaks at a rally on Capitol Hill in 1984 to seek support for legislation that ultimately made it illegal for people under age 21 to purchase and possess alcohol.

MOTHERS AGAINST DRUNK DRIVING (MADD)

In May 1980, 13-year-old Cari Lightner was walking to a school carnival when a drunk driver lost control of his car and hit Cari and killed her. When the driver was arrested, the police found out that he had already been convicted of driving drunk three times. He had also hit another person with his car just two days earlier; he was out on bail when he killed Cari.

Cari's mother, Candy Lightner, was furious. She couldn't understand why a man with a long history of drinking and driving wasn't in prison. At the time, however, there were no laws in place to keep drunk drivers in jail. Lightner decided to put the anger she was feeling to good use: She started an organization called Mothers Against Drunk Driving (MADD).

Five years after Cari's death, 50 states had made their drunk driving laws much stricter, thanks to the efforts of Candy's groups. "The goal of MADD was to reduce drunk driving traffic fatalities and the organization has been highly effective in raising public disapproval of drunk driving," writes sociology professor David J. Hanson. "The proportion of traffic fatalities that are alcohol-related has dropped dramatically, in part because of MADD's good efforts."

WAYNE COWDEN: USING ANGER TO BE A BETTER ATHLETE

In 1990, Wayne Cowden was a student at Pennsylvania State University and a top athlete on the college's gymnastics team. Because Wayne's father had also been a competitive gymnast, Wayne grew up under great pressure to be the best in his sport. Although he trained hard and developed his natural talent, he really started to achieve success after he came up with a new technique to inspire himself when he had to perform: getting angry.

Wayne said, "I get angry with myself before I compete," reported college journalist Dana Pennett in the university's student newspaper the *Daily Collegian*. "I psych myself out, not in a negative way. I just go out there and do it for myself and if something goes wrong, I know who to blame." Wayne explained that when he was younger, he would be very nervous before a gymnastics meet. To overcome that nervous energy, he learned to use anger constructively to help himself feel strong. He explains that it is tremendously important to focus when doing a routine on the rings and also when trying to achieve goals. Wayne described his technique, saying that you "set new goals all of the time.

And when you don't meet those goals, something's wrong. That's when you have to get angry with yourself and push for that extra little bit."

Clearly, anger can be an excellent force for change. As psychologist and anger management trainer Tony Fiore writes, "Anger can be a good thing if it gets us past fear and paralysis and catapults us into appropriate action." It can give you the energy you need to stand up for yourself and the things you believe. In order for anger to be a positive force, however, you need to understand how to harness its power.

7

MANAGING FRUSTRATION AND ANGER

Character isn't inherited. One builds it daily by the way one thinks and acts, thought by thought, action by action. If one lets fear or hate or anger take possession of the mind, they become self-forged chains.

—Helen Gahagan Douglas (1900–1980), U.S. politician

By now, it should be clear that anger is something everybody experiences—it can't completely be avoided. What *can* be controlled is the way you respond to your anger and the way you express it. Controlling anger isn't easy. In fact, there is an entire specialty in the field of psychology called anger management that focuses on teaching people how to deal with their frustration and anger. This chapter will take a look at some of the techniques that anger management experts recommend.

WHY IS ANGER MANAGEMENT IMPORTANT?

You have the option of letting loose every time you feel angry, shouting or even lashing out in violence at the people who made you mad. What's wrong with that? The answer is: a lot of things. For one, uncontrolled anger can take a serious toll on your health. As health writer Melissa Tennen explains, "Anger causes the body to react like it's under attack, kicking the sympathetic system into gear." The sympathetic nervous system controls the body's fight-or-flight reaction, which increases the stress level in the body. Researcher Redford Williams mentions some specific health risks that are related to anger, saying, "It's pretty clear that a lot of people who are angry . . . are the people at higher risk for a heart attack. . . ."

Anger can also cause problems in your relationships with friends and family. In her 2007 book, *All About You*, Dorothy Kolomeisky writes, "Some ways of dealing with anger are destructive and hurt relationships. Anger can even ruin a relationship if a person allows his or her temper to get out of control." If, when you get angry, you scream at the person who triggered your anger, hold a grudge against the person, or explode and punch or throw things, it is easy to see why people might not want to be your friend. Although you might think lashing out in anger helps you get your way, it's probably not true. "Anger often backfires," explains Marc Deiner in the September 2006 issue of *Entrepreneur Magazine*. "You just never know how the other side will react. Anger may drive . . . [your opponent] to sabotage you later. And if your opponent carries a grudge, pray you never need anything from him again."

Being viewed as an angry person can also hurt you when it comes to school or work. It's hard for people to respect someone who flies into a rage and can't control his or her emotions in public. Anger can actually cost businesses money. As psychologist and anger management expert Dr. Tony Fiore explains, "Workplace anger is costly to the employee, the company, and coworkers. Studies show that up to 42 percent of employee time is spent engaging in or trying to resolve conflict. This results in wasted employee time, mistakes, stress, lower morale, hampered performance, and reduced profits. . . ." Everyone benefits by learning to control anger and channel it in order to get work done or to fulfill goals.

ANGER MANAGEMENT

As was previously discussed, anger is not only an emotion; there are physical symptoms that go along with it. "A burst of anger takes 90 seconds to come and go, unless you choose to rethink the thoughts and restimulate the response," says scientist Jill Bolte Taylor in the August 2008 issue of *Psychology Today*. In other words, every time you get angry, you can feel better in just a minute and a half—so long as you let go of angry thoughts and move on. If you keep thinking about whatever it was that made you angry, your anger can continue.

Learning how to stop dwelling on your anger is just one part of anger management. In order to deal with anger, you first need to know what makes you angry and how you get angry. This will help you find the anger management technique that will work best for you.

Anger management is a field that has been growing for decades, if not centuries. "The effort to develop acceptable outlets for anger . . . forms an important thread in modern American history," according to anger management experts Carol Zisowitz Stearns and Peter N. Stearns. Because most people are nervous around excessive or violent displays of anger, they have become "unusually sensitive to expressions of the emotion when they do occur," Stearns and Stearns say. As a result, anger management has become a very popular—and necessary—field. Many companies, schools, and other organizations provide anger management training for their employees, students, and members.

ANGER MANAGEMENT TECHNIQUES
Examine Your Anger

Therapist and stress management expert Elizabeth Scott believes that the best way to handle anger in a constructive way is to take a good look at your anger and what is causing it. Sometimes when you get mad at something or someone, you may not realize that there are deeper reasons behind your anger. "Sometimes people may feel generally irritable because of stress, sleep deprivation, and other factors," Scott writes. "Once you are more aware of your sources of anger, you can take steps to deal with it."

It also helps to talk about anger with a trusted friend or family member. However, Scott cautions that talking about one's anger can sometimes lead a person to dwell on the things that make him or her angry. This only extends the anger and makes it worse. Ideally, Scott says, "It's best to talk about a situation only once, exploring solutions as well as your feelings."

Managing Anger in the Moment

When something makes you mad, it can be hard to think clearly. That's why it's so important to learn anger management techniques *before* you get angry. That way, you'll have the tools you need when that angry moment comes along. In *All About You*, Dorothy Kolomeisky outlines several actions you can take to cool your anger and learn how to handle it in a way that protects your health and your relationships. These actions include the following:

* Stop where you are, breathe deeply, and count to 10. Don't say or do anything until you have taken this step.
* Think about what might happen if you let your anger loose. If you're in school, you could risk getting in trouble or being suspended. Consider whether expressing your anger is worth suffering the possible consequences.
* Calm down. Walk away from the situation and take a little while to get control of yourself.

* Think about other ways you might be able to express your anger besides yelling, hitting, or saying mean things about the person who made you angry.
* Do your best to put yourself in the place of the person who made you angry. Think about what the person's motivation was for doing whatever it was that made you angry. You might realize that the whole situation is just a misunderstanding.
* Talk about your anger. Try to forgive the person who made you angry and, if possible, explain to him or her why your feelings were hurt and you became angry.
* Get help from someone you can trust, such as a teacher, parent, or guidance counselor. There are many people who can support you as you learn to manage your anger.

Other Techniques

One of the most popular and easiest techniques for controlling anger is deep, calm breathing. Most people don't realize that the way they normally breathe is shallow and doesn't bring as much oxygen into their bodies as they really need. Taking the time to stop and focus on breathing deeply and slowly, filling up your lungs completely, can go a long way toward relieving anger. Over the long term, deep breathing also works against the stress that can help spark anger.

Meditation takes the calmness you get from deep breathing a step further. It allows you to relax deeply by clearing the distracting and stressful thoughts from your mind. Dr. Herbert Benson of Harvard University explains that a regular meditation practice "typically results in reductions in stress, short temper, headaches, backaches, insomnia, cholesterol levels, blood pressure, hyperventilation, anxiety, and panic attacks. . . ." It can also help you learn to exercise control over yourself when you get angry.

THE LIFE SAVERS TECHNIQUE

In his book *Anger Management for Dummies*, psychologist W. Doyle Gentry mentions an interesting method of controlling anger. He calls it the Life Savers technique. Simply put, you keep hard candy, such as Life Savers, nearby all the time. Then, pop one into your mouth when you get angry. Before you allow yourself to react to the person or situation that's making you angry, you have to wait until the entire piece of candy has dissolved. As Gentry explains, this technique works for several reasons:

* From the time people are infants with bottles and pacifiers, they have an instinct that makes them feel safe and calmer when they suck on something.
* The sugar from the candy causes chemical changes in the brain that make a person feel pleasure, which helps overcome his or her anger.
* It takes around five minutes for a piece of hard candy to dissolve, so this gives a person time to calm down and to think about how best to respond to a tense situation. Also, a person can't scream and shout in anger when there is a piece of candy in his or her mouth.

Gentry gives an additional piece of advice: "Don't bite the Life Savers. It defeats the purpose of the exercise by shortening the length of time before you act on your anger and, more important, by indulging your aggressive personality."

Developing a better sense of humor is another great way to keep your anger in check. As anger management experts Glenn Schiraldi and Melissa Hallmark Kerr explain, "Humor changes our perspective on life. It breaks the grip of fear and pain, expanding our outlook to optimism, acceptance, fun, and play. It is difficult to feel powerless when we feel alert and amused. . . ." As has been discussed, anger is often related to feelings of powerlessness. By giving you back your sense of power over your life, humor makes it easier for you to get past your anger and move forward.

Psychologist W. Doyle Gentry offers many possibilities for ways to ease anger. For one, stay away from drugs and other substances such as nicotine and alcohol, which can make you more likely to get angry. It is also a good idea to not take in too much caffeine, for the same reason. Gentry also emphasizes the importance of getting enough sleep and trying to overcome stress. By taking care of your health, you can take care of your anger—and vice versa.

You can also use your imagination and daydreams to help you control your anger. All you have to do is close your eyes and imagine being somewhere you love, such as the beach or the mountains. Picturing yourself in your special place can help you escape from the place you really are, even if the escape is only for a little while.

In the end, it doesn't really matter what healthy technique you use to manage your anger. It's only important that you *do* manage it, so you don't risk hurting yourself, others, or your relationships.

GLOSSARY

abolitionist   A person who works to end slavery

adrenaline   A hormone that stimulates the body

assertive   Strong and self-assured, but not violent or aggressive

bipolar disorder   A mental illness in which the person's mood swings from depression to mania, a state where the person feels excited and energetic but may be irritable

borderline personality disorder   A mental illness in which the person has unstable moods and problems with relationships and self-image

cardiovascular system   The heart and blood vessels that supply blood to the parts of the body

cognitive   Relating to thinking or one's thoughts

concentration camp   A place where prisoners are confined and often harmed

delegate   A representative at a meeting

ghetto   A poorer part of cities where members of a particular ethnic group live, whether by choice or by force

glucose   A form of sugar that the body uses for energy

grassroots   At a local or community level

Holy Land   The area that was Palestine in ancient times. This area has religious meaning for Jews, Christians, and Muslims.

hormones   Chemicals found naturally in the body that speed up or slow down different body processes

militant   Aggressive or tending to be violent

neurotransmitter   A chemical messenger found in the brain

paranoid   Believing that others are out to get you

passive-aggressive   Showing negative feelings in ways that aren't outwardly angry, such as being stubborn or procrastinating

provocation   A trigger, or a thing that makes someone angry

ratify   To include as an official part of the U.S. Constitution

scapegoat   Someone or something that is blamed for the problems of others

schizophrenia   A mental illness in which the person experiences hallucinations, confusion, and problems functioning in everyday life

sympathetic nervous system   The system in the body that tends to increase the heart rate and slow down other functions, such as digestion

BIBLIOGRAPHY

The African American Registry. 2006. Available online. URL: http://www.aaregistry.com. Accessed September 18, 2008.

"The American Civil War: Introduction." History.com, 1996. Available online. URL: http://www.history.com/minisites/civilwar/viewPage?pageId=628. Accessed September 18, 2008.

American Psychological Association. "Controlling Anger— Before It Controls You." APA Online, 2008. Available online. URL: http://www.apa.org/topics/controlanger.html. Accessed September 18, 2008.

American Psychological Association and World Science Staff. "Behind School Shootings, Rejection and Anger." *World Science*, August 20, 2007. Available online. URL: http://www.world-science.net/othernews/070820_cynical-shyness.htm. Accessed September 18, 2008.

"Anger." Kids' Health. Available online. URL: http://www.cyh.com/HealthTopics/HealthTopicDetailsKids.aspx?p=335&np=287&id=1728. Accessed September 18, 2008.

"Anger and Health." Anger Alternatives, 2007. Available online. URL: http://www.anger.org/?nav=health. Accessed September 18, 2008.

"Anger Fact Sheet." British Institute of Anger Management, 2008. Available online. URL: http://www.biam.org.uk/index.php?option=com_content&task=view&id=13&Itemid=10. Accessed September 18, 2008.

"Anti-Apartheid Struggle." GlobalSecurity.org, 2005. Available online. URL: http://www.globalsecurity.org/military/world/war/south_africa1.htm. Accessed September 18, 2008.

Barcus Miller, Kate. "Anger Management: Anger Issues and Types of Anger." Ask the Therapist, 1998. Available online. URL: http://www.askthetherapist.com/counseling archive-types-of-anger.asp. Accessed September 18, 2008.

Barker, Phil. "Anger." BeyondIntractability.org, September 2003. Available online. URL: http://www.beyondintractability. org/essay/anger. Accessed September 18, 2008.

Becourtney, Lyle. "Anger Can Be Positive." Ezine Articles, August 18, 2007. Available online. URL: http://ezinearticles.com/ ?Anger-Can-Be-Positive&id=691535&opt=print. Accessed September 18, 2008.

Bohlin, Karen E., and Bernice Lerner, eds. *Great Lives, Vital Lessons: A Character Education Curriculum Resource for Grades 5–8*. Boston: Boston University's Center for the Advancement of Ethics, 2005.

Bond, Annie B. "The Dalai Lama's Wisdom About Anger." Care2, August 11, 2005. Available online. URL: http://www. care2.com/greenliving/the-dalai-lama-s-wisdom-about-anger.html. Accessed September 18, 2008.

Bousman, Gary. "Anger: It Can Be Like Slow-acting Poison, Robbing You of Mental and Physical Health." *Vibrant Life*, July 1, 1995. Available online. URL: http://www.encyclopedia.com/ printable.aspx?id=1G1:17000739. Accessed September 18, 2008.

Chadha, Pradeep. "Anger—What It Does to the Body." Ezine Articles, February 9, 2006. Available online. URL: http://ezinearticles.com/?Anger--What-It-Does-To-The-Body&id=14281&opt=print. Accessed September 18, 2008.

Channing L. Bete Company. "What Is Anger?" 1985. Available online. URL: http://www.jcfcc.vcn.com/anger.html. Accessed September 18, 2008.

Chow, Ellesse. "Inspirational Stories IV: Helen Adams Keller, A Great Heroine." Goal Setting College, 2008. Available online. URL: http://www.goal-setting-college.com/inspiration/ hellen-adams-keller. Accessed September 18, 2008.

Cline, Austin. "Causes, History, and Violence of the Crusades." Agnosticism/Atheism, 2007. Available online. URL: http:// atheism.about.com/od/crusades/a/crusades_4.htm?p=1. Accessed September 18, 2008.

Cline, Austin. "Perspectives and Religion in the Crusades." Agnosticism/Atheism, 2007. Available online. URL: http://atheism.about.com/od/crusades/a/crusadesviews_4.htm?p=1. Accessed September 18, 2008.

"Coaching Center—The Effects of Anger." 2006. Available online. URL: http://www.gocampus.org/modx/index.php?id=192. Accessed September 18, 2008.

Cutler, Howard C. "The Mindful Monk." *Psychology Today*, May/June 2001. Available online. URL: http://psychologytoday.com/articles/index.php?term=pto-20010501-000021&print=1. Accessed September 18, 2008.

Danitz, Tiffany. "Bullying Contributes to School Shootings, Report Says." Stateline.org, October 25, 2000. Available online. URL: http://www.stateline.org/live/ViewPage.action?siteNodeId=136&languageId=1&contentId=14154. Accessed September 18, 2008.

Davis, Mike. "Vigilante Man." TomDispatch.com, May 6, 2005. Available online. URL: http://www.tomdispatch.com/post/2378/mike_davis_on_the_return_of_the_vigilante. Accessed September 18, 2008.

DeAngelis, Tori. "When Anger's a Plus." *APA Monitor on Psychology*, March 2003. Available online. URL: http://www.apa.org/monitor/mar03/whenanger.html. Accessed September 18, 2008.

Dentemaro, Christine, and Rachel Kranz. *Straight Talk About Anger*. New York: Facts on File, 1995.

Diener, Marc. "Using Anger as a Negotiating Tactic." *Entrepreneur Magazine*, September 2006. Available online. URL: http://www.entrepreneur.com/article/printthis/165944.html. Accessed September 18, 2008.

Dyson, Michael Eric. "The Prophetic Anger of MLK." *Tikkun*, April 4, 2008. Available online. URL: http://files.tikkun.org/current/article.php?story=20080406073548643. Accessed September 18, 2008.

Erb, Scott. "Comparative Politics: Terrorism." Available online. URL: http://academic.umf.maine.edu/~erb/classes/2cp3.htm. Accessed September 18, 2008.

Fable, Jan Luckingham. "Historical Anger Gets in the Way of Living a Day at a Time." Forhealing.org, 1997. Available online. URL: http://www.forhealing.org/anger.html. Accessed September 18, 2008.

Fiore, Tony. "Five Lessons About Anger Being a Good Thing." Ezine Articles, July 13, 2006. Available online. URL: http://ezinearticles.com/?Five-Lessons-About-Anger-Being-a-GOOD-Thing&id=242976&opt=print. Accessed September 18, 2008.

Fiore, Tony. "The High Costs of Anger in the Workplace." *Holistics Living*, 2004. Available online. URL: http://1stholistic.com/reading/health/A2004/health-the-high-costs-of-anger.htm. Accessed September 18, 2008.

Foster, David. "10 Ways Angry People Change the World." Davidfoster.tv, March 4, 2008. Available online. URL: http://www.davidfoster.tv/?p=691. Accessed September 18, 2008.

Fuchs, Cynthia. "I Am an Animal: The Story of Ingrid Newkirk and PETA." *PopMatters*, November 19, 2007. Available online. URL: http://www.popmatters.com/pm/reviews/51102/i-am-an-animal-the-story-of-ingrid-newkirk-and-peta/print. Accessed September 18, 2008.

Gandhi, Arun. "Passive Violence Fuels the Fire of Physical Violence." Victory Over Violence, 1998. Available online. URL: http://www.vov.com/experiences/gandhi.html. Accessed September 18, 2008.

Gaylin, Willard. *The Rage Within: Anger in Modern Life*. New York: Simon & Schuster, 1984.

Gentry, W. Doyle. *Anger Management for Dummies*. New York: Wiley Publishing, 2007.

Greenpeace. "About Us." Available online. URL: http://www.greenpeace.org/usa/about. Accessed September 18, 2008.

Griffin, R. Morgan. "It's a Mad World." WebMD, April 30, 2007. Available online. URL: http://men.webmd.com/features/

what-does-anger-do-to-your-health?print=true. Accessed
September 18, 2008.

Hanh, Thich Nhat. *Anger: Wisdom for Cooling the Flames*. New
York: Riverhead Books, 2001.

Hanson, David J. "Mothers Against Drunk Driving: A Crash
Course in MADD." Alcohol Abuse Prevention. Available
online. URL: http://www.alcoholfacts.org/CrashCourse
OnMADD.html. Accessed September 18, 2008.

Harmeling-Benne, Hope. "Historical and Cross Cultural
Perspectives on Anger." Available online. URL: http://
w3.salemstate.edu/~hbenne/ids/anger.pdf. Accessed
September 18, 2008.

Harmon, Shirley. "How to Use Anger Constructively—
Managing Anger, Part 1." Find Articles, February 1992.
Available online. URL: http://findarticles.com/p/articles/
mi_m3230/is_n2_v24/ai_12073279/print. Accessed
September 18, 2008.

Hill, James, and Jaime Hennessey. "Kevin Everett: 'He Is a
Tiger.'" ABC News, January 31, 2008. Available online.
URL: http://abcnews.go.com/print?id=4216671. Accessed
September 18, 2008.

"Hostility, Anger Linked to Chemical That May Cause Heart
Disease." *Science Daily*, May 1, 2000. Available online.
URL: http://www.sciencedaily.com/releases/2000/05/0005
01081252.htm. Accessed September 18, 2008.

Ignatius, David. "Young Anger Foments Jihad." *Washington Post*,
September 13, 2006. Available online. URL: http://www.
washingtonpost.com/wp-dyn/content/article/2006/09/12/
AR2006091201298_pf.html. Accessed September 18, 2008.

"Information About Anger." The Anger Management Centre.
Available online. URL: http://www.angermanagement
centre.ca/info.html. Accessed September 18, 2008.

Irving, James. "Avoiding School Shootings." Family Education,
2008. Available online. URL: http://life.familyeducation.
com/school-safety-month/violence/36339.html. Accessed
September 18, 2008.

Johnson, Bill. "Terrorism." Probing Islam. Available online. URL: http://www.probing-islam.org.uk/terrorism.htm. Accessed September 18, 2008.

Kelly, Martin. "Top Five Causes of the Civil War." American History. Available online. URL: http://americanhistory.about.com/od/civilwarmenu/a/cause_civil_war.htm. Accessed September 18, 2008.

Kelly, Martin. "Top 9 Events That Led to Civil War." American History. Available online. URL: http://americanhistory.about.com/od/civilwarmenu/tp/secessionevents.htm. Accessed September 18, 2008.

Knickerbocker, Brad. "Arson and Death Threats Have Followed Ecoterrorists' Call for More Use of Force." *The Christian Science Monitor*, September 26, 2002. Available online. URL: http://www.csmonitor.com/2002/0926/p01s01-ussc.htm. Accessed September 18, 2008.

Kolomeisky, Dorothy, with Myra Stanecki-Kozlowski and William Haines. *All About You: A Course in Character for Teens*. Charleston, S.C.: BookSurge Publishing, 2007.

Limon, Connie. "Is Being Angry Ever Good?" Positive Articles. Available online. URL: http://www.positivearticles.com/article.php?id=7973&act=print. Accessed September 18, 2008.

"Lincoln and the Republicans." World Book Encyclopedia and Learning Resources. Available online. URL: http://www.worldbook.com/wb/Students?content_spotlight/civil_war/lincoln. Accessed September 18, 2008.

Long, Roderick T. "Thinking Our Anger." *Formulations*, Summer 2001. Available online. URL: http://libertariannation.org/a/n03012.html. Accessed September 18, 2008.

Loo, Tristan. "Anger Management." 2005. Available online at http://www.synergyinstituteonline.com/forms_bank/1200767918.PDF. Accessed November 5, 2008.

———. "What Causes Anger?" August 9, 2005. Available online at http://ezinearticles.com/?What-Causes-Anger?&id=58598. Accessed November 5, 2008.

Lumpkin, Andrew. "Typologies of Religious Violence." Amazon.com, June 1, 2005. Available online. URL: http://www.amazon.com/Sacred-Fury-Understanding-Religious-Violence/dp/0759103623. Accessed September 18, 2008.

Marshall, Henrietta Elizabeth. *This Country of Ours: The Story of the United States.* New York: George H. Doran Company, 1917.

Mayo, Edith P. "An Introduction to the Women's Suffrage Movement." National Women's History Museum. Available online. URL: http://www.nmwh.org/exhibits/helpdesk/exhibit_text.html. Accessed September 18, 2008.

Meyer, Cathy. "Four Ways to Keep Your Anger from Causing Physical Illness." Divorce Support, 2007. Available online. URL: http://divorcesupport.about.com/od/angerandconflict/tp/anger_physillness.htm?p=1. Accessed September 18, 2008.

Nanda, B.R. "Gandhi and Non-Violence: Doctrines of Ahimsa and Satyagraha." Infinity Foundation. Available online. URL: http://www.infinityfoundation.com/mandala/s_es/s_es_nanda_ghandi.htm. Accessed September 18, 2008.

National Health Service. "Anger." First Steps. Available online. URL: http://www.firststeps-surrey.nhs.uk/anger.htm. Accessed September 18, 2008.

"Nonviolent Action—Philosophy: Dr. Martin Luther King." AKidsRight.org. Available online. URL: http://www.kids-right.org/p_martin.htm. Accessed September 18, 2008.

North, Sean. "Thousands of Failures, but Thousands of Patents." Ezine Articles, March 17, 2005. Available online. URL: http://ezinearticles.com?Thousands-of-Failures,-but-Thousands-of-Patents&id=20906&opt=print. Accessed September 18, 2008.

O'Brien, Kerry. "Exclusive Interview with the Dalai Lama." *The 7:30 Report*, December 6, 2008. Available online. URL: http://www.abc.net.au/7.30/content/2007/s2273196.htm. Accessed September 18, 2008.

Pennett, Dana. "Cowden Uses Anger to Get Higher Scores." *The Daily Collegian*, March 8, 1990. Available online. URL: http://www.collegian.psu.edu/archive/1990/03/03-08-90dsports-01.asp. Accessed September 18, 2008.

"PETA's History: Compassion in Action." PETA Media Center. Available online. URL: www.peta.org/factsheet/files/FactsheetDisplay.asp?ID-107. Accessed September 18, 2008.

Pierce, William. "Focusing Our Anger: To Be Effective, Our Anger Must Be Properly Directed." *Free Speech*, May 1997. Available online. URL: http://www.natvan.com/free-speech/fs975b.html. Accessed September 18, 2008.

"Professor: Shooter's Writing Dripped with Anger." CNN.com, 2007. Available online. URL: http://edition.cnn.com/2007/US/04/17/vtech.shooting. Accessed September 18, 2008.

Pynn, Kyle. "Patriots in the American Revolution vs. ' Terrorists' in Al Qaeda." Helium, 2002. Available online. URL: http://www.helium.com/items/464156-patriots-in-the-american-revolution-vs-terrorists-in-al-qaeda/print. Accessed September 18, 2008.

Radio National. "Distant Mirrors, Dimly Lit: Anger." *Distant Mirrors, Dimly Lit*, July 25, 2003. Available online. URL: http://www.abc.net.au/rn/learning/lifelong/stories/s858195.htm. Accessed September 18, 2008.

Rosenwein, Barbara H. *Anger's Past: The Social Uses of an Emotion in the Middle Ages*. Ithaca, N.Y.: Cornell University Press, 1998.

Rubin, Theodore Isaac. *The Angry Book*. New York: Collier Books, 1969.

Santella, Andrew. "All the Rage." *The Utne Reader*, Summer 2007. Available online. URL: http://www.utne.com/print-article.aspx?id=9614. Accessed September 18, 2008.

Schiraldi, Glenn R., and Melissa Hallmark Kerr. *The Anger Management Sourcebook*. New York: McGraw-Hill, 2002.

Scott, Elizabeth. "Do's and Don'ts of Dealing with Anger." Stress Management, May 5, 2008. Available online. URL:

http://stress.about.com/od/stresshealth/a/dealing_anger.
htm?p=1. Accessed September 18, 2008.

Sharma, Vijai P. "Anger Can Exact a Heavy Price." Mind Publi-
cations, 1996. Available online. URL: http://www.mindpub.
com/art083.htm. Accessed September 18, 2008.

Sierra Club. Available online. URL: http://www.sierraclub.org/
inside. Accessed September 18, 2008.

"Social Issues: The Holocaust, The Shoah." *NW Travel Magazine
Online.* Available online. URL: http://www.u-s-history.com/
pages/h1677.html. Accessed October 20, 2008.

Speck, Gary B. "A Trail of Hope." Ancestry.com, January 1, 2003.
Available online. URL: http://freepages.history.rootsweb.
ancestry.com/~gtusa/trails/mormon.htm. Accessed September 18, 2008.

Stearns, Carol Zisowitz, and Peter N. Stearns. *Anger: The
Struggle for Emotional Control in America's History.* Chicago:
The University of Chicago Press, 1986.

Sutter, Tim. "Salem Witchcraft: The Events and Causes of
the Salem Witch Trials." Salem Witch Trials, 2000.
Available online. URL: http://www.salemwitchtrials.com/
salemwitchcraft.html. Accessed September 18, 2008.

Tennen, Melissa. "Angry People Hurt Their Hearts." Health
A to Z, June 2007. Available online. URL: http://www.
healthatoz.com/healthatoz/Atoz/common/standard/
transform.jsp?requestURI=/healthatoz/Atoz/hc/men/life/
alert07272004.jsp. Accessed September 18, 2008.

Thomas, Sandra P. "School Connectedness, Anger Behaviors,
and Relationships of Violent and Nonviolent American
Youth." FindArticles, 2004. Available online. URL: http://
findarticles.com/p/articles/mi_qa3804/is_200410/ai_
n9484280. Accessed September 18, 2008.

"The Turbulent 1850s: A Prelude to War." Afro-American
Historical Association of Fauquier County, 2007. Available
online. URL: http://www.aahafauquier.org/Inside AAHA/
Museum/VirtualMuseumAPreludetoWar/tabid/86/Default.
aspx. Accessed September 18, 2008.

United States Senate. "The Caning of Senator Charles Sumner." Available online. URL: http://www.senate.gov/artand history/history/minute/The_Caning_of_Senator_Charles_ Sumner.htm. Accessed September 18, 2008.

Webber, Rebecca. "Me Search." *Psychology Today*, August 2008, 76–84.

Zackery, Robert T. "Anger Management FAQ: The Good, the Bad, the Ugly." MayoClinic.com, June 26, 2007. Available online. URL: http://www.mayoclinic.com/health/anger-management/MH00075. Accessed September 18, 2008.

FURTHER RESOURCES

Block, Joel D., and Fred J. Block. *Staying Cool: How to Get a Grip on Anger*. Issaquah, Wash.: Wellness Institute, 2002.

Carlson, Richard. *Don't Sweat the Small Stuff for Teens*. New York: Hyperion, 2000.

Covey, Sean. *7 Habits of Highly Effective Teenagers*. London: Simon and Schuster, 2004.

Crist, James J. *Mad: How to Deal With Your Anger and Get Respect*. Minneapolis, Minn.: Free Spirit Publishing, 2007.

DiConsiglio, John. *Out of Control: How to Handle Anger—Yours and Everyone Else's*. New York: Franklin Watts, 2008.

Wilde, Jerry, and Kara M. Webb. *More Hot Stuff to Help Kids Chill Out: The Anger and Stress Management Book*. Richmond, Ind.: LGR Publishing, 2000.

Web sites

American Psychological Association: "Controlling Anger Before It Controls You"
http://www.apa/org.publicinfo/anger.html
This site provides lots of information about the causes of anger and how to control it.

Anger Management: Get Your Angries Out!
http://www.angriesout.com
This site takes a light-hearted approach to anger management, and contains interesting information for kids and adults.

KidsHealth
http://kidshealth.org
This site provides information on all kinds of health-related issues for kids and young adults.

Mayo Clinic

http://www.mayoclinic.com/health/anger-management/MH00073
This site teaches how to examine the deeper reasons why we get angry and how to manage anger in healthy ways.

PICTURE CREDITS

Page:

INDEX

ABOUT THE AUTHOR AND CONSULTANTS

Tara Tomczyk Koellhoffer earned a degree in political science and history from Rutgers University. Today, she is a freelance writer and editor with more than 12 years of experience working on nonfiction books, covering topics ranging from social studies and biography to health and science. She has edited hundreds of books and teaching materials, including a history of Italy published by Greenhaven Press and the *Science News for Kids* series published by Chelsea House. She lives in Pennsylvania.

Series consultant **Dr. Madonna Murphy** is a professor of education at the University of St. Francis in Joliet, Illinois, where she teaches education and character education courses to teachers. She is the author of *Character Education in America's Blue Ribbon Schools, First & Second Edition* and *History & Philosophy of Education: Voices of Educational Pioneers*. She has served as the character education consultant for a series of more than 40 character education books for elementary school children, on the Character Education Partnership's Blue Ribbon Award committee recognizing K-12 schools for their character education, and on a national committee for promoting character education in teacher education institutions.

Series consultant **Sharon L. Banas** was a middle school teacher in Amherst, New York, for more than 30 years. She led the Sweet Home Central School District in the development of its nationally acclaimed character education program. In 1992, Banas was a member of the Aspen Conference, drafting the Aspen Declaration that was approved by the U.S. Congress. In 2001, she published *Caring Messages for the School Year*. Banas has been married to her husband, Doug, for 37 years. They have a daughter, son, and new granddaughter.